Outwit

College

Professors

*An insider's
guide to
secrets of
the system*

John Janovy, Jr.
Fifth Edition

**With a contributed chapter by Nicole
Searcey, champion outwitter**

2015

Designed by John Janovy, Jr.

This book was previously published by: Pearson Education, Inc.
(2nd Edition)

ISBN-10: 151697963X

ISBN-13: 978-1516979639

A request to the readers of this book:

Please let me know via e-mail that you've found this book useful; be sure to put OUTWIT as the subject line so I won't delete your message. Good luck in college. I wish you all the success in the world. May you always get the right kind of instructors, and if you eventually get filthy rich, I hope you give generously to the academic programs of the college that gave you your excellent education.

Also, if you have tricks or ideas that you would like to contribute to the next edition, you can send those to me via e-mail: jjparasite@hotmail.com. If you do send a suggestion then it is understood that I have complete permission use that suggestion without charge and without compensation in all future editions in all media, including electronic, and all languages throughout the world. So don't send anything unless you agree to those terms. If you send something then indicate whether you want, or will allow, your name attached to it. I can credit you in two ways: mention you in the text itself (Jane Doe finds that if she . . . etc.) or I can include you in an acknowledgements chapter. Either way is fine with me, but you need to tell me your wishes.

For regular mail, my address is:

John Janovy, Jr.
School of Biological Sciences
University of Nebraska Lincoln
Lincoln, NE USA 68588-0118
www.johnjanovy.com

—JJJr

[iii]

This book is dedicated to all those students who were participants in our Friday afternoon coffee house sessions. Looking back, it really was a good idea; my special thanks to Ben Hanelt for the original suggestion.

This book is also dedicated to the nearly 20,000 students to whom I have given grades since September 1, 1966, and especially to those who worked in my laboratory and told me endless horror stories about their various profs.

Outwitting College Professors

Table of Contents:

Num	Dept	Title	Cr	Grade
109	CHEM	Gen Chem	4	C+
101	BIOL	Gen Biol	3	C
101L	BIOL	Gen Biol L	1	D+
150	ENGL	Comp	3	C+

1. Why You Need to Outwit Your Prof

Nature teaches beasts to know their friends.

—W. Shakespeare (*Coriolanus*, 1607)

There are three basic reasons why you need to outwit your college professors, and here they are:

(1) College professors can, and usually do, have a lot of control over your life and your future. In general, anyone with power over you needs to be outwitted. Profs have power because they issue grades in courses for which you pay lots of tuition. But they also have much power to recommend you for scholarships, write good letters of recommendation, and provide interesting experiences that you can talk about to impress dates and people who might be interviewing you for a job.

(2) College profs usually are far busier than most people think although that busy-ness often concerns activities that many people—especially those engaged in real business—think are pretty dumb. Nevertheless, professor busy-ness takes their minds off things that are important to you. So you need to get them back on track. You need to get them thinking about your welfare instead of some deadline imposed by their department

administration. That is, you need to get them working for you instead of for their own bosses.

(3) College professors live in a paradoxical world because they are among the most intellectually free people on Earth, but they also operate under a massive burden of regulation, compliance, and rules for behaving properly so their institutions won't get sued. They usually need help living in this world, although most of them don't know it. You can provide such assistance. Your interactions with them can soothe the irritations caused by rules and regulations, relieve the frustration resulting from academic politics, and make their job a satisfying one. In theory, they should reward you for such favors by opening doors for you. Maybe one of those doors will be at a fine medical school or law school.

Control over your lives:

Although college professors don't have *complete* control over your life, they have enough power so that they need to be taken fairly seriously. You have plenty of control over what happens in college classes, too, so unless you plan to use your own skills and efforts to advance your career, then give this book to a friend and go get a job. The advice in this book is given with the assumption that you're already doing everything you can to succeed in college, and perhaps feel like you're doing okay, but maybe think you need a little bit of an advantage over the system.

If you're a D student then *Outwitting College Professors* is not going to make you an A student. If you're a solid B student, however, there's a pretty good chance this book will help you turn into a B+ student, and in some cases even an A student. This book probably will be most helpful, however, if you make a lot of C grades, mainly because such students usually have the most potential for change.

I'll admit right up front that not everything in this book pertains directly to outwitting college professors. It turns out that the behaviors you need in order to outwit one of these people will actually turn you into a better college student and help you to succeed out in the world after you leave college. This book could be entitled *How to be a Better College Student* and it would contain some of the same advice it does now, but it would not be nearly so much fun to read and the advice would not seem so devious. If you've been to the movies lately, you know that deviousness can be quite entertaining and educational. So I've put the boring advice (how to be a better college student) toward the end and tried to stick to the more interesting material (how to outwit your prof) in the main part of the book.

College professors control almost everything that happens in class, including lecture presentations, handouts, pictures, words, assignments, quizzes, and exams. You don't have much power to offset this type of control, so just accept it. You may not like what you hear and see in class, but it's not the prof's responsibility to make you like it. His or her only responsibility is to make it legitimate.

If this person is at all aware of his or her reputation on campus, he or she will also try to make you like whatever happens in class. But remember that this is only a prof, not a standup comic, no matter how much he or she may try to act like the performer. So let the person control that over which he or she has absolute power, and decide going in that you are going to control those things over which you have power (see also the boring chapter on how to be a better college student).

Control over classroom behavior:

What college professors generally can't control is who enrolls in their classes and how those students behave once they've enrolled, although the more advanced the class, the more likely the students will be a rather select group. But by the time you get into advanced classes, chances are you've already mastered many of the techniques in this book anyway, or are smart enough not to need them very much, so that your classmates don't represent an opportunity to outwit your profs.

In introductory courses, however, and especially ones with relatively large numbers of students, your classmates' behavior usually represents a major opportunity for outwitting your instructor. Although college professors try to keep things calm by threatening pop quizzes or requiring attendance, the real truth is that they have little if any control over student behavior in a large introductory course.

Recently, however, so-called classroom response technology has become the vogue and this technology provides a prof quite a bit of power over your behavior. Classroom response ("clicker") systems consist of pads that resemble TV remotes and allow or require students to answer questions anonymously, the results being displayed for all to see. If your prof uses this kind of system, your first rule is to *never lose your clicker, always have fresh batteries in it, and always bring it to class.*

The second "clicker rule" is to figure out how to get it registered properly the first time and do it. You're not outwitting anyone by doing these things, but enough of your classmates will violate these rules so that you have a slight advantage over them and appear, in the eyes of the prof, as a responsible citizen.

The more high-tech instructional equipment that is in your large introductory classroom, the less likely you will be able to stand out, mainly because technology can have a dehumanizing effect on people and in an educational setting it can quickly become a means for your prof to keep you at a distance.

On the other hand, institutions may have invested in "interactive classrooms" filled with technology. Profs who use such classrooms skillfully will design a lot of small exercises that are intended to use various learning modes: writing, drawing pictures, exit questions, small-group problem solving, etc. Such profs are just asking to be outwitted, but quite frankly, they're doing most of the outwitting work for you because their various learning activities are intended to be engaging. Regardless of the prof's teaching style, or the classroom setting, in order to outwit one of these folks you almost always need to stand out from the crowd in a positive way.

For example, if your fellow students must be told to put away their phones and newspapers, get their feet off the chairs, and be quiet, you're in business. If the prof has to tell people to put away their phones and newspapers twice in the first four days of class then you're really in business. Simply sit somewhere in the front one fourth of the classroom, sit up straight, have your notebook open and ready to take notes, pencil in hand, and stare at the prof with wide open eyes. It's not very difficult.

On the other hand, sometimes a problem can turn into a positive experience. Not long ago, standing in front of a large auditorium full of freshman students, three ladies in the back of the room simply would not shut up, and the laughing seemed to be disturbing those around them. So I kicked them out of class. As you can imagine, the other 257 people in that room were very attentive for the rest of the period. But I got an e-mail later that day from one of those who'd been sent out:

> JJ - I was asked to leave your class this morning and I just wanted to say that I am sincerely sorry for my actions. I am ashamed

and I honestly meant no disrespect to you or my classmates. Make no mistake, I was very humiliated by being asked to leave class. I really was paying attention to your lecture and final exam preparation discussion, but I did allow myself to become momentarily distracted and I take full responsibility for that lapse of judgment. Please understand that I am not writing this in order to argue my actions as acceptable, because I was in the wrong, but I just wanted to tell you that I am sorry. Respond if you wish, but I just thought you should know.

I responded. And the fact that this student sent the above message means that at the end of the semester, if she is a tenth of a point away from the next highest letter grade, I'll move her up. But the real lesson is that no matter how anonymous or hidden you may think you are in a large auditorium, a teacher can probably see you and recognize immediately whether you are contributing to the overall academic atmosphere or being a distraction to your classmates. Fifty minutes is not very long. Just sit there, pay attention, and at least look like you're taking notes, glancing up at the screen or blackboard periodically, even if you're busy writing a poem or a letter to your significant other.

Sound simple? It is simple. In fact, it is so incredibly simple that after a few days you'll find yourself wondering why so many of your classmates are doing exactly the opposite behavior. In this case, your prof is trying to control the group, usually by intimidation, threat, or some other coercive means, but you're sitting there knowing that the very behavior that disturbs him or her is allowing you to come across as a serious student. Once this prof knows your name, and can recognize you out on the campus sidewalks as well as in the first few rows of some large auditorium then you've made major progress and about the most you can hope for is that your classmates continue acting like they need a couple of years in the army before trying college.

Control over your conversation:

Regardless of the subject, college classes usually involve a large amount of information that is relatively important for a variety of reasons. First, it may be essential to your understanding of a subject that is directly applicable to your chosen profession. If you are a pre-med, for example, taking a physiology course then kidney and heart function are directly applicable to your career. Second, course content may be important for you in your role as a citizen of a highly technological and complex society. Regardless of your major, history and literature both help you become a better citizen, make more intelligent decisions in the voting booth than you might if you were ignorant of the past or of human passions, and guide your children when they need help with perspective and values.

Most students don't understand this second reason, and a great many of them just don't believe this reason is valid. You are not a "most student." You understand the most important reason why course information is of value mainly because it gives you something to talk about besides sports, weather, and your friends.

In a couple of other places in this book I mention conversation about topics other than those that consume the talking time of so many people. This advice is repeated because it's one of the easiest and most effective ways to outwit a prof. If you are serious about outwitting this person who has so much power over you then decide immediately that you are going to build your conversational repertoire day by day, adding topics, ideas, concepts, information a-bout the arts and literature, history, and interesting places you'd like to visit. You never know when one of those sub-jects will become a highly effective means of influencing your prof's opinion of you as a student, or the opinion of a potential employer after college.

In general, faculty members and students tend to walk the same sidewalks, visit the same businesses near campus, attend the same athletic and cultural events, and often eat in the same student union. Thus you are always likely to en-counter one of your teachers outside the classroom. Thirty seconds in one of these situations, and thirty words about something other than the weather, sports, and your friends, or your grades, are often more than enough to make a big difference in the way your prof thinks about you.

Information from classes can also be quite useful on dates, especially if you're a guy going out with a very smart coed who is likely to get admitted to medical or law school and end up earning a six figure salary. Although this book is about outwitting college professors, not dates, some of the same techniques work—for men—with dates because so many guys act like children regardless of the social situa-tion. Act like a grown up with something to say about the world and your date is likely to be impressed, especially if you act like a gentleman, too.

If you're female, I'd suggest using information you've learned in class in a fairly judicious manner, depending on the guy and your interest, or lack thereof, in him. If you are female then most and maybe all of you know exactly what I'm talking about, so I won't elaborate.

College professor busy-ness:

Most college profs hate busy-work with a passion but are constantly preoccupied with it because of their job. You may believe that you are intruding, or taking up their valuable time, but in fact they're most often just looking for any excuse not to be doing whatever happens to be making them look so busy. Never feel uncomfortable interrupting a college professor. Most will welcome it unless they are under a real deadline. Statistically speaking, however, college professors are rarely under such deadlines, so showing up at their office usually is a welcome relief.

You can also just ask your prof "Is this a good time?" But remember, profs are just like people from off the street or in an airport terminal. They are a sample of humanity, so some will be pleasant and cooperative and others will be sullen and maybe even tell you to go away. If one tells you to go away, I recommend asking if there is a better time. Any prof who tells a student, "No, there is no good time," is asking for trouble with his or her supervisor and knows it.

One student suggested I add a comment about how to talk to a teacher who has no respect for you, and is difficult to even engage in a conversation. Well, some of my colleagues are just like that, and I've never solved the problem of people with no interpersonal skills. They do, however, reveal how important it is for *you* to acquire such skills. Some of the advice in chapter 10 ("Advanced Outwitting") will apply to a situation in which you have to deal with such a person. I also suggest reading Nicole's letter to her young relatives (chapter 12); her advice to those children will help even a college student deal with difficult people in professional settings.

If a prof is persistently ugly about meeting with students then I also recommend telling all your friends about this individual's sullenness. Eventually some students will complain to that prof's boss, and if such complaints occur often enough, the faculty member will be in official trouble. That teacher's reputation will start to suffer and eventually he or she may get disciplined for mistreatment of students, perhaps by not getting a raise some year.

[9]

This conflict may not get resolved to your satisfaction, but it's a lesson in life. In extreme circumstances, you can always write to a member of the school's governing board, your state legislature, or your student newspaper. If nothing else comes of this kind of experience, you will get some practice writing persuasively, and such practice is always helpful in other classes. But the real bottom line is that the vast majority of college professors welcome any legitimate interruption from busy-ness imposed by the system, especially when that interruption is an interesting one. So your challenge is to immediately go beyond the apologetic stage and acquire some intellectual weapons that profs might find interesting.

The paradoxical world of college professors:

I call the world of college professors "paradoxical" because it is filled with contradictions and conflicting obligations. Most profs must be productive scholars, yet they are not necessarily hired to do that. At smaller schools they are definitely hired to teach but many still want to do research of some kind although their time and resources for independent study may be severely limited. Thus there is a constant battle for their intellectual energies. The subject area that made them want to become a prof in the first place, that intriguing body of knowledge and mystery that sustains their life of the mind, usually conflicts with the basic job for which they were hired.

So you must understand that even during what seems like a perfectly normal conversation, a prof's mind might well be a million miles away. Your first task is to bring the prof's mind back to reality, back to why he or she is having this conversation with you in the first place. Later chapters contain some tricks for accomplishing this task, but for the moment, remember the reason for needing to outwit this teacher: you want his or her mind focusing on *you* instead of on some little insect, a chemical reaction, or the Battle of

[10]

Bull Run. Your goal is to make this activity we call teaching an interesting and satisfying one for your prof. If you can accomplish this goal, you have suddenly gained some control of the student-prof relationship, and in most cases, a lot of control.

College professors are perhaps more free, intellectually, than any other people in American society except for the retired and wealthy. By intellectual freedom, I mean the freedom to think whatever they want to think, occupy their minds with about any subject, take any side of an argument just for the sake of exercising their brains, and write papers or books about almost anything. In this regard, profs are quite different from most corporate employees who must be in tune with company goals, especially financial ones, sales and marketing strategies, and their bosses' approaches to business. On the other hand, profs also try to get *you* to think in a certain way. So their goals for you are in contradiction to their goals for themselves. Profs therefore need to be outwitted so you can learn to be an independent thinker without damaging your career.

Although college professors are intellectually free, they are not at all free from a variety of other kinds of constraints, including behavioral, ethical, financial, and regulatory ones. If they don't treat you with a certain amount of respect by keeping you at a reasonable distance then they're likely to find themselves in violation of workplace ethics, maybe even to the point of getting sued or dismissed.

If the prof is a scientist at a larger institution then he or she is saddled with all kinds of regulatory burdens such as chemical inventory, hazardous materials paperwork, safety training, etc. If the prof is in the humanities, his or her library needs usually are a constant source of frustration. If the prof is in the arts, practice and studio time always compete, and sometimes very strongly, with teaching, although studio classes and individual lessons are teaching that involve something the prof has little control over, namely the amount of time and effort *you* spend practicing.

All of these professor types need to be fooled into believing, even if for only a short time, that whatever they are doing to help you advance *your* career and life is more important than whatever they are doing to advance their own careers and personal lives. In other words, they need to feel good about taking time away from themselves and giving it to you. This book is your guide to helping them accomplish such a feat.

Final take-home message:

You need to plan your interactions with college professors rather carefully for many valid reasons. Most of these reasons have nothing to do with your own abilities and interests, but instead concern the profs' professional lives and workplace environments. Thus most of what happens between students and profs should never be taken personally. Instead, interactions should be analyzed within the context of a professor's job. You should see yourself as a helper instead of a subject. This altered vision is the first step toward a successful outwitting endeavor and, of course, a better looking résumé, great letters of recommendation, and, eventually, a lucrative career.

2. Know Your Foe

We are not enemies, but friends. We
must not be enemies.

> —Abraham Lincoln (*First In-*
> *augural Address, March 4,*
> *1861*)

Before actively engaging in any contest of the wits, you must know the individual you're trying to outwit. Although your prof is not really a foe or an enemy, he or she is not necessarily a friend, either. Most college professors learned long ago that students are a highly varied bunch and so in their minds success as a teacher takes equally varied forms. Not all "A" students are considered success stories; not all "D" students are failures, at least to a teacher. So the first thing you need to know is that your prof judges you differently than you judge yourself.

You are most likely to measure your own success in terms of a grade. Your prof measures it in terms of what he or she thinks you learned, regardless of your grade, and he or she usually measures you in term of how honestly you tried to learn the subject being taught. Your first goal, therefore, is to appear progressively more and more educated as the semester passes, regardless of your grade, and most certainly to *appear* more concerned about your education than about your transcript.

[13]

College professors are also people, i.e., human beings, typically with car payments, mortgages, children, sometimes grandchildren, marriages, divorces, pets, interests in sports, and hobbies. In other words, they're about like the general population except that they tend to care a little less about money and more about ideas than the average person on the street. On the other hand, colleges and universities provide havens for people whose personalities are not necessarily compatible with the business world, and occasionally this incompatibility is extreme.

A short list of the worst cases is given below. If you can find some other wacko types, let me know and I'll add them to the next edition. Unless your prof obviously falls into one of the following three categories then he or she is probably fairly close to normal and can be dealt with using the techniques described in the first nine chapters of this book. However, if you recognize this person in the next three numbered paragraphs, and especially if this individual has any serious power over you in a college or university setting, then be sure to consult the "Advanced Outwitting" chapter. One rule that applies to the following three types is to never (*never!*) ask one for a letter of recommendation.

DANGEROUS TYPES, BEWARE:

1. The terminally insecure prof:

This person is dangerous but probably does not realize it at all because he or she is often delusional to boot. These folks are manipulative spoiled brats, always having to be right and always having to stand in judgment of those over whom they have power. There are *lots* of these types in academia and they can be real bullies. If you encounter one of these, or believe you have, consult chapter 10, "Advanced Outwitting," immediately. You'll get the warning if none of the material in the first nine chapters seems to apply, or, especially, when your gut reaction is one of fear, distrust, and a sneaking suspicion that "something" is just not right.

2. The feminist female/lecherous male:

Any prof that exhibits obvious gender bias—positive or negative—is a problem for students of the opposite sex and sometimes of the same sex. The first time you encounter one of these types, turn immediately to chapter 10 and study it carefully. You might actually find that these folks are pretty easy to outwit, at least compared to first type mentioned above. Once you get into the workplace, you'll probably discover the same kinds of people, maybe a lot of them, so consider your encounter as a student to be a fairly educational experience. But also consult chapter 10.

3. The really incompetent prof with no interpersonal skills (and burnt-out cases):

More of these inhabit the hallowed halls of academia than you realize. Most students give their profs a whole lot more credit than many of them deserve, the main reason being that students need decent grades on their transcripts and besides, even a burnt-out case has been studying the material for decades so knows a lot more about it than do the students. Thus the prevalence of this type is usually greatly underestimated. Routinely I hear students talking about profs like this, but in mildly irritated terms, or sometimes even in amusement. Encounter with an incompetent burnt-out case is not nearly the crisis that a terminally insecure type produces; consult chapter 10 at your leisure.

Aside from these three difficult types, everyone else is mostly like the average person, but be sure to remember that often they are very interested in ideas and events rather than in money and other people (you may find this gentle reminder several places in this book). They also like to talk about ideas and events, even ones outside their own discipline, in which case they may or may not be talking about something they know anything about.

Because profs tend to live in their minds, there are some general subjects that will probably work to increase your chances of getting a better grade. If you'll learn enough about these topics to at least start a conversation, or respond to any opportunity to show you know anything about them then you'll make an impression. Usually the "enough" is not very much, so this is no PhD course on the Protestant Reformation or quantum mechanics. I'll reveal some of these topics in later chapters (see the section on accessories, for example, in chapter 3). You'll also get better educated by learning to talk about them, but that's not the point. What we want to do is outwit a college professor, successfully, and if getting better educated is part of the price, consider it a small price indeed. But back to the subject of knowing your foe.

Office visits:

Always visit your profs in their offices early in the semester, and if you can do so during their office hours, so much the better. They've already decided that office hours are wasted time so it doesn't bother them much to use it talking with you. But statistically speaking, students who visit profs during their office hours are a distinct minority because so few actually do it. Thus whenever you walk in you're actually doing this person a favor, making his or her time somewhat less of a waste, and bolstering his or her ego a little bit. And if you ask for legitimate help, you're bolstering that ego a lot.

The first thing you should do upon entering a college professor's office is to introduce yourself. It's okay to extend your hand; he or she may actually shake it. If there is a chair that looks like it's intended for visitors, it's okay to sit in it without being asked; nobody is going to tell you to stand up. It's okay to take off your coat or jacket, but it is necessary to do it in a special way, depending on the season and whether you're male or female. If you're a male, take it off outside the office and carry it in; if you're a female visiting a male professor, wait until you sit down to take off your coat, but if it's a female professor, take off your coat outside and carry it in. College students are old enough, and have watched enough television, to figure out in a hurry why this coat-removal body language, picked up from daytime TV, works.

The second thing you should do is study the furnishings and decorations, although don't be too obvious about it. Pictures of wives, children, and pets should always be noted, as should photographs of special places and scenes. Posters are clearly a key to a person's interests, and a framed poster is an especially important indicator. For example, a framed Chicago Bulls poster makes a very different statement than one advertising a Picasso exhibition.

Furnishings themselves—desks, chairs, stools, computer tables, curtains or shades, rugs or carpet—anything that is not institutional issue should be noted. You can tell in a moment from furnishings whether your prof considers his or her office an extension of home, and if so, then respecting it as such will always earn points. If that assertion seems strangely foreign to you, ask your mom for some advice about what to look for and how to respect it, or ask her to repeat the advice she already gave you when you were growing up.

The third thing to do is study your prof's library; they all have them and their libraries are strongly indicative of interests and personalities. Art and literature books in a scientist's office reveal a major vulnerability to being outwitted because this person is already an uncomfortable stranger in his or her department and will welcome your

[17]

outwitting efforts, possibly even recognizing them for what they are and enjoying them. So the general rule about libraries is: look for anything that is outside the prof's immediate discipline or area of professional interest. That "anything" is what nobody, or at least very few immediate colleagues, talk about to this individual, even though he or she may be vitally interested in the "outside" subject. If you see such art or literature, you've just been dealt an ace.

This first office visit or two is when you acquire the basic information you need to outwit this person, so try to notice anything that will serve as a conversational opener when you see your prof at a social occasion or outside of class, for example at the student union, a local bar, or an athletic event. In addition to pictures, if there is music playing or a stereo in the office, then notice what that music is. You may not want to learn anything about Mozart or Bach, but hey, if it helps you with a grade, then that's not many brain cells wasted.

If you don't recognize the classical music then cock your head, listen a moment, and ask what it is. Smile and act appreciative when told, although if you're told in a tone of voice that implies you're an idiot for not knowing the famous blah-blah from blah-blah then consider this individual a candidate for chapter 10. But if this person says, in a gentle, communicative way, something like

"Oh, that's Mozart's *Trumpet Concerto in D*," then the proper response is

"It sounded familiar; my mother always listens to Mozart."

Obviously the next time you're in that office you can tell this professor that you mentioned to your mother that Mozart's *Trumpet Concerto in D* was playing in his or her office and that your mother and father were greatly impressed. Profs love it when taxpayers are impressed with classical music, but if your folks hate music in general, you may have to keep them away from this prof at graduation ceremonies.

Telephone conversations:

There are two situations you need to know about. The first is when you're in a prof's office and the phone rings; the second is when you call this professor. The first situation is very easy to deal with. If you're in a prof's office and the phone rings, get up and stand outside the door so that this conversation can be conducted in what your prof believes is in private. Of course it's usually not private at all, but that's probably not a whole lot of use to you. It's entirely possible, however, that this individual is involved in something borderline ethical, or hotly political (in an academic sense), or in a conflict with the system. If it's the latter, then you've been tossed another ace; all you have to do is complain about the system yourself when given an appropriate chance (without mentioning you've overheard the conversation), and you'll score a bunch of points.

As for calling the prof, don't do it unless for some reason you believe it's okay. For example, if he or she has listed a phone number on the syllabus, that's a signal that it's alright to call. If the prof gives a home phone on the syllabus, he or she is just asking to be interrupted almost 24/7.

When you call your prof, always start by stating your full name, slowly, and asking if he or she has time for a phone call. If the answer is "yes," then have a specific question or request ready, again speaking directly into the receiver and fairly slowly. DO NOT call your prof from a noisy bar with your cell phone about to lose its charge. If you get an answering machine then it's even more important to state your full name slowly, and the return call number, also slowly, and twice if you can, especially if this prof is older than fifty.

[19]

When a prof calls back, use correct grammar: "This is she (he)," not "This is her (him)." The very next sentence should be "I called you because . . ." and have a good reason. If you end up making an appointment then keep it; if you can't keep it, call or e-mail at least an hour ahead of time. All these simple rules are violated so often by students that the ones who follow them stand out in a very positive way. In other words, when it comes to outwitting profs, at least in telephone conversations, simple business conversation using correct grammar is of major importance.

Of course like much of the advice in this book, whatever it takes to outwit your prof may also serve you very well in other places after college and with other people but again that's not the real reason we're developing these skills. We want to outwit a college professor and get you a better looking transcript.

Students also have answering machines or services, and if you're going to call a prof and leave a number on his or her answering machine then be absolutely certain that your own "hello" message is clear, calm, dignified, and neutral. Hello messages that have a bunch of loud music playing in the background, or are mumbled rapidly in a high-pitched voice, create an immediate negative impression on an older caller. So if you naturally have a squeaky voice and talk real fast then turn off the music and get a slow-talking low-voiced friend to record the answering machine message.

The Outwittability Profile (OP):

Photocopy this checklist and make a copy for each of your profs. Then take them to class the first week of the semester and fill them out, either in class or immediately afterwards while your memories are still fresh. Rate each item from one to ten; it's okay to adjust your ratings over the week, but try to get them finalized within four class days.

You'll end up with an OP score and an OP profile. You're going to plot this profile and formulate your outwitting plan depending on how the line looks.

1. Dress, from complete slob (0) to sport coat and tie (10).

2. Where he/she looks during class, from at the blackboard or screen, or over your heads (0) to directly at the students, making sure he/she scans the whole audience (10).

3. Lecture notes, from hand written in pencil on legal pads (0) to non-existent (10).

4. Visuals, from drawing or writing on whiteboard, chalkboard or overhead in small scribbles (0) to a carefully orchestrated mixture, ranging from extemporaneously sketched scenes or characters to slick PowerPoints with lots of pictures, cutesy arrows, and circles (10).

5. Speech, from mumbling and breaking off sentences (0) to talking in complete paragraphs (10).

6. How he/she answers a student question, from arrogant or disdainful know-it-all (0) to friendly and respectful, usually by either repeating a question for the benefit of the class, or saying "that's a good question," or both (10).

7. Whether he or she is fumbling and helpless with instructional technology (0), or so skillful and adept at manipulating the multimedia facilities that you hardly are aware of them (10).

8. How much stuff he/she carries to class regularly, from a large bag of some kind (0) to very little, maybe a CD, a flash drive, or a folder (10).

9. Whether he/she manages time well, from being totally oblivious to time and running over (0), to keeping an eye on the clock so that each class is brought to some kind of a closure, provides a few minutes for ques-

tions, and gets out on time, even a minute or two early (10).

10. Whether handouts are carefully counted or given to each student (0), or given out in big handfuls or stacked on a table, so that students have to either pass them around or pick them up themselves (10).

11. Whether he/she has a web page with nothing at all about teaching on it, other than maybe classes listed (0), to at least some text about what his/her courses are all about, some of the activities, etc. (10).

12. Whether he/she has any kind of an outside scholarly activity or independent research, from none (0) to at least some that he/she talks about a little bit (10).

Now plot your cumulative rating points, being sure to keep the items in the order they are listed. A perfect 10 on all items will produce a straight line from zero to 120, with the resulting line having a slope of 10 (an increase of 10 units for each item). This is the easiest prof of all to outwit, simply because he or she expects it, and even enjoys it or wants it, knowing full well that you're becoming a better college student because of your outwitting efforts.

Departures from a straight line with a slope of 10, whether they be concave, convex, or simply have a lower slope present a challenge, and the greater the departure, the more of a challenge. In general, the straight lines that end at values lower than 120 reveal a fairly predictable individual, with one ending at zero being the burnt-out case (see chapter 10). If a straight line ends at 60, then this person is average in every way and may respond in an average way to your outwitting efforts. Large departures from straight lines present complex but interesting cases; most of these are dealt with in chapter 10.

What to do with the OP:

The answer to this question depends a great deal on the profile's shape, but for now, the best thing to notice is whether the line is relatively straight or not, and if so, whether its end point (final score) is high or low. If the end point is high, anywhere over 100, feel free to use all the outwitting tricks suggested in this book and to devise some of your own. If the relatively straight line's end point is between 40 and 100, then try all the tricks, but do them in an increasingly subtle way the lower the final score. If the end point is below 40, then find a way to use the suggested tricks in a very gentle, almost sympathetic, non-threatening way and think about adding something about history to your repertoire (unless the class subject is history, then the repertoire should contain something about the history of science, music, or art). Burnt-out cases usually remember something in the past that was pleasant or rewarding, so a trick that uses history is often effective.

Suggestions:

If you have other ideas or suggestions, please send them along. I'll have them evaluated by a small panel of students, probably on a Friday afternoon down at the Indigo Bridge Coffee House, and if there is consensus that the suggestions are worth trying, I'll put them in the next edition, with acknowledgments of their source unless you wish to remain anonymous, so please tell me if that's the case.

But if you send me a college prof story, you are consenting to have your submission published in the next edition, and perhaps all subsequent editions, of *Outwitting College Professors*. You will not be paid or compensated for your submission and I may edit it for clarity and space considerations. Nevertheless, thanks in advance! And if you're a former student of mine and have used some outwitting tricks on me, tricks that now appear in this book, I greatly appreciate your past efforts. You did indeed make a positive contribution to American higher education whether you intended to or not!

Final take-home message:

Study each prof and develop some kind of an outwittability profile, whether it's of the type mentioned above or one of your own invention. Profs can vary quite a bit, so adjust your tactics to the kind of person who has control over your grades and recommendations. If you have specific suggestions, and are willing to share them then send them along with a permission to use them, without compensation, in all future editions of this book in all languages and media, including electronic, throughout the world.

3. Dress and Appearance

She wears her clothes, as if they were
thrown on her with a pitchfork.

—Jonathan Swift (*Polite*
Conversation, ~1738)

Clothes and grooming send a message and we all know it. We live with this fundamental truth about humans every day. All of us choose our clothing in order to tell others something about ourselves. We also respond to what others are telling us about themselves by their dress, hairstyle, and accessories. College professors are no different in this regard than college students. The mistake most college students make with college professors, however, is that of assuming their professors don't notice what students are wearing. College profs usually are quite aware of your personal appearance and clothes because that's the only information we have about you—what you look like when you walk into class or through our office door. So whether you realize it or not, clothing is one of your most effective means of outwitting people like me.

Here are some clothing and appearance tricks that I know students have used to help solve this problem of uneven distribution of power—profs with lots, you with little. Although the tricks in this chapter deal mainly with appearance, they may also be used effectively in combination with others, for example those mentioned in chapter 4, "Small Talk/Big Talk."

Some of these tricks may work for you, and if you have good ones to add to the list, great. But I know that these work because they've been used on me for years. The first thing a student must do is study the prof like he or she was a book over which there's a big exam tomorrow. The second thing you must do is learn the six basic dress and appearance tricks and use them in a way that fits your prof's OP (Outwittability Profile; see chapter 2).

The six basic tricks:

1. Start with that section of the syllabus where the prof tells you something about himself or herself. This information is often as important as whatever is in the text. It's also the place where the prof is telling himself or herself that he or she belongs in front of this class; that is, it's a little bit of an ego trip, thus a statement of what this teacher likes to think he or she has accomplished in academic life. Such syllabus information is best interpreted in terms of the prof's dress and appearance.

   Professor clothing is a dead giveaway because it tells you whether this person cares anything at all about appearance and grooming. If it seems like this is the case then he or she links a professional appearance with scholarly activity. But if your prof dresses like a slob then this person lives a life of the mind—completely. Slob dress in front of a classroom tells you this person's spouse doesn't know or care about appearance, either. Many profs have web pages; be sure to check these out and glean any kind of information from them about what this person really likes. Chances are excellent that whatever information he or she provides to the world online is also information you can use to your benefit.

2. Take some notes on your prof's first few days in front of the class. Is she highly organized? Does he walk from side to side? Is posture important, or even a part of the overall message? Does he wear a tie? Does she take care of her hair? What kind of lecture notes does she use? Does he crack jokes, or at least try to? Does he laugh at his own jokes? Does she throw in comments about subjects other than the one she's teaching in order to put the lecture material into a broader context, or does she stick strictly to he subject? How old is this person? The answers to these questions will form the basis for your outwitting strategy. If you visit this person in his or her office, you will need to dress in a way that matches both the style and self-image of your instructor.

3. Remember that this individual with power over you also is studying you from the front of the room. You are neither anonymous nor invisible regardless of how convinced you are that is the case. Your prof knows where you prefer to sit, with whom you prefer to sit, and whether you take notes. He or she also knows something about your wardrobe and hairstyles. If the class starts before 10:00AM, he or she knows whether you take a shower and get dressed with some consideration for your appearance, or stay up late, sleep in, and throw on whatever's lying around just to cover up your body.

Depending on fashion trends, your prof may well know all about your tattoos, even those in places people would normally keep covered up, because college students as a group tend to be less covered up than say lawyers or insurance salesmen on the job, especially in warm climates or seasons. Most profs pass judgment, especially on women, based on how much skin is showing or how self-conscious they are about that skin. I suspect that if you took a national poll of college professors who teach freshman courses, you'd probably discover that a surprising fraction of them know which coeds wear Victoria's Secret stuff, simply because so many of them show it off constantly, at least in warm weather. So if you're going to show a lot, don't be self conscious about it, or flaunty in front of the opposite sex.

4. Remember that anything distinctive or unusual about you is an aid to a teacher who might be at all interested in knowing who you are. Some profs have no desire to learn your name, but that's their problem and it's costing them money and reputation, even as you're reading this paragraph. Others believe it is vitally important to be able to put a name with a face, even to the point of taking pictures of their students. Professors who try to learn their students' names, especially in very large classes, acquire a reputation that serves them well in the cloistered arena of academic politics.

Students, however, are often afraid that profs will learn their names and so try hard to remain anonymous. *This fear is a real mistake*. In order to outwit a college professor you must make sure he or she knows you and can recognize you on the street. Then use that knowledge to your advantage. Your clothing and appearance are truly major weapons in this outwitting game. If, for example, the prof's syllabus or web page says she got her PhD from the University of Oklahoma then wearing an OU sweatshirt to class four or five times will get you remembered instantly.

5. If you're a female, look in the mirror and assess what you see, evaluating that image within the context of society's standards for young women. This recommendation may seem like a sexist one, but you ladies do it a thousand times a day anyway, and will do it

every day for the rest of your lives, so admit it and use the knowledge to your advantage.

If you're really gorgeous, drop-dead beautiful—at least as judged by the obviously artificial standards you see on television and on the magazine racks at any local grocery store then you have a problem. If you see nothing but ugliness in the mirror, too much fat, bad skin, and unruly uncooperative hair, you have another kind of problem. Fortunately, it's easier for you to solve the latter problem than the former.

Why is this difference the case? Because if given a choice of companions, even for a few minutes of casual conversation, most profs choose brains over beauty. He or she can tell in an instant whether you've been treated like a gorgeous babe—and nothing more—all your life. If you have, then you're more of a teaching challenge than you ought to be. Maybe later I'll expand on that assertion, but for the moment, remember that extreme physical beauty is not always an advantage in every circumstance. But talk that sounds like you have brains, or at least are using the one you do have, will always make a positive impression on profs, *always*.

On the other hand, if your male prof easily recognizes that you're not Miss America then that's to your distinct advantage because neither is his wife and even if he cares what you look like—which he probably does not—then he's likely to be sympathetic. Your female prof is at least ten times as perceptive as your male prof, and if you're a beauty queen then you represent competition and that's the biggest problem of all. Your female prof is far more likely to see you as a threat than your male prof is to see you as an object of desire. Most coeds believe exactly the opposite. But in either case plan to dress accordingly whenever you know they are going to see you.

There's only one kind of clothing that's best to a-void, at least at public universities, and that is a sweat-shirt or t-shirt with anything religious on it, including the name of a denominational high school. It's also important not to wear clothing with any other univer-sity's logo or name on it (unless, of course, your prof went there and you actually know something about the school).

Such types of clothing are a problem, especially for women students, because they suggest a less-then-clean mental slate. Another university's logo on a sweatshirt could well mean that you have a significant other at the faraway school, thus may not have your mind com-pletely on calculus or European history. On the other hand, men who wear t-shirts or sweats with another uni-versity's logo are usually considered to have picked up the stuff at a garage sale or the Salvation Army.

If you tell a public university professor, by what-ever means, including your clothing, that you have at-tended an ultraconservative religious academy, that prof will immediately assume your mind probably is closed to certain ideas—e.g., evolution—whether it really is or not. Closed minds are anathema to profs, so if you have one, or carry other major distractions like a serious sig-nificant other far away, hide it well.

6. If you're a male, there is one so-called "rate-limiting" trick to outwitting your prof, and if you don't use this one then all your other efforts are likely to either be in vain or have diminished effectiveness. Here's the trick: *get up early enough to do something with your hair and leave that damned cap at home, especially if you plan on wearing it backwards.* A backwards cap sends a message that's reasonably non-academic. I can't ex-plain why this happens; it just does whether it's justi-fied or not.

The second piece of advice for males is to make sure you can speak the English language with simple grammatical rules in place. I don't know why males tend to use incorrect grammar more than females, and maybe my 46 years of college teaching and 20,000 grades awarded don't represent a good sample. But I can assure you that one of the quickest ways to create a bad impression on any teacher is to say "I've went . . ." or use the non-word "alot" in a written assignment. A chapter on dress may not seem like the best place to talk about grammar, but clothes and speech go together, and a male student who comes in to a faculty office wearing his cap on backwards and saying "I've went . . ." will never get the benefit of the doubt if his grade is borderline.

After having solved these two preliminary problems, the "cap syndrome" and the "wrong verb plus 'alot' syndrome," for males the rest is very easy. If you're smart enough to make a C on your own then acting smart enough to make a B will help you get there. Be able to talk about two concepts typical of the course subject, be able to talk about two subjects peripheral to the course but in the news, and read a couple of important books about history and politics. If given any opportunity whatsoever, talk about these ideas, subjects, and books in the presence of your prof (again, see chapter 4).

If you can have even a two minute conversation, especially in the company not only of your prof but also of another student who can't or won't accomplish this relatively simple task then you're on the way to a higher grade, especially if you're wearing conventional or semi-conservative clothing: at least clean jeans and an intact t-shirt with your secular high school logo on it (but no cap) and carrying an interesting book which

[31]

you've at least started to read. Anything more dressy is a plus, within reasonable limits; you don't want to look so good it's out of character. You're also on your way to a better college education by acting this way, but that's by default instead of on purpose.

Accessories:

Accessories are always an important part of one's appearance. Every woman knows this basic rule, but few men do, and even fewer care. College women often make the mistake of thinking that accessories are important only for social occasions away from class or campus, when items like purses, shoes, jewelry, cell phones, etc., are all part of the equipment with which women compete with other women. College men tend to view accessories as a big pain in the rear that they have to carry, although some rabid outdoorsy types tend to reveal that part of their character with backpack and shoe design. But accessories can be a vital part of your outwitting equipment and should be used regularly. They're as much a part of your dress as your jeans.

Here are some accessories recommended for encounters between university students and faculty, regardless of gender or college: Mozart or Bach CDs, books like Karen Armstrong's *The Battle for God* and Samantha Powers' *A Problem from Hell: America in a Century of Genocide*, sheet music (so long as it's complex and you have a good story about why you're carrying it), current liberal magazines such as *The New Yorker, Harpers, Art in America,* or *The Atlantic Monthly*, musical instruments in their cases (if you actually play one in the band or orchestra), sketch pad or other art supplies (provided you have a couple of nice sketches in the pad, no matter how primitive), a camera of about any kind, your laptop, a textbook for another course (especially if it's history or philosophy), or a pretty leaf or flower that you might have picked up on campus.

Here are some student accessories that are to be avoided at all costs during such encounters: personal music containers, *especially* if you still have the ear plugs in, athletic equipment, large crosses hanging around your neck (small, tasteful, and subtle crosses are okay, especially on women), Bibles, knives, guns, and other weapons, plastic bags filled with anything, and chemistry texts.

These recommended lists of do's and don'ts are preliminary ones, and they're based primarily on the stereotypical makeup of faculties at mid-sized to large public universities, especially those in or near large cities. A high percentage of such faculty members are fairly liberal and analytical, and they usually read widely. These characteristics do not make them evil, but they do tend to shape their judgments, including subliminal judgments about students who might be on the borderline, grade-wise. If you're on the borderline then a subjective impression of how hard you're trying, whether you actually are or not, could easily influence your grade.

Cell phones are a special problem. My advice is to use them out of sight most of the time, and especially out of hearing range, of your prof. A coed who pulls her phone out and connects with a boyfriend the instant class ends, babbling personal talk within hearing range of everyone, or walking down a campus sidewalk yakking and laughing, is a student whose mind is not on her academics. A male student who does the same thing is even in worse shape in terms of faculty opinion because of the stereotypes society has of supposedly strong men in control of business. So put your phone away, especially in class.

On the other hand, coming into a prof's office and conspicuously turning your phone off and putting it deep into your back pack is good behavior, guaranteed to help make you look like a serious student. If your prof sees you walking down the sidewalk *without* a phone, looking at campus plants, studying building architecture, or doing similar things that reveal curiosity then you've scored a few points, especially if the people around you are oblivious to their surroundings and consumed with inane conversations everyone else can hear, and *especially* if you look up and say "hi" to the prof. Trust me; it's easy.

Advanced phone use, however, allows you some options, especially within earshot of profs. If you're a female student, then some four-letter language gives the impression of having an open mind and not being particularly bound by convention or stereotype, especially if you're using this language in reference to some ultraconservative closed-minded politician. If you're a male, avoid the four-letter language at all costs and be overheard talking about a concert or planning a study session in the library. In either case, being overheard discussing some normal obligation that you have to meet (have to be at work at a certain time, your car is in the shop, clothing at the cleaners, etc.), is a conversation that makes you appear responsible, especially if carried out in a calm, businesslike, tone.

And remember, with smart phones you don't really have to be talking to anyone to make a good impression; your prof just needs to *think* you're actually talking to someone. You can always appear to turn the thing off, smile, and say something like "that was my mom; she always wants to send me cookies or know if I'm coming home for Thanksgiving" (for female prof) or "that was my dad; he wants to surprise my mom on her birthday" (for male prof).

What to look for in faculty offices:

After mastering the six basic wardrobe and accessory tricks above, it's time to step up a level. If you find yourself in a faculty office, and you should, at least twice, maybe three times a semester, then your options for outwitting grow considerably. Most profs consider their office an extension not only of themselves, but also of their homes. If a male teacher dresses carefully, usually wearing a coat and tie, especially if the tie is actually tied and his shirt collar buttoned, you can predict that his office will be organized and carefully arranged. If a female teacher dresses carefully then her office is likely to be somewhat less carefully arranged, at least on the surface, but she'll consider it arranged in an important way. In either case, don't come in and touch or move anything.

Male profs are more likely to have offices that are absolute messes than are female profs. If a male prof's office has papers and books scattered everywhere then it's probably okay to move some in order to sit down. He has to search for stuff whenever he wants it anyway, and probably considers the search entertaining, so you're actually helping if you move a book out of a chair so you can sit. If the place is an absolute pit, then a casual comment like "oh, it's just like my dorm room" instantly creates empathy.

If the prof is female and has pictures of her family, focus on the children. If it's a male prof and he has pictures of his family, focus on his wife, unless there are children who obviously are grandkids then focus on them. Saying something complementary about these respective people ("She's so pretty." or "They're so cute." for wives and children or grandchildren respectfully) will work to create a positive impression every time.

Final take-home message:

Decide that dress and appearance, including accessories, do make a difference in faculty-student relationships, and plan accordingly, especially if you know that you'll encounter your prof. This knowledge allows you to plan encounters that seem casual but actually are a part of a careful strategy for making a professor see you in a positive way, as a serious scholar. Such an impression never hurts, and can only help your grades.

You don't know whether you're going to end up at the end of the semester exactly on a borderline between two grades. If you've played your cards right, that prof could easily simply move you up to the next highest grade because you've created the right impression. There's no guarantee this move will occur, but you're not looking for guarantees so much as increasing your statistical chances of making this move happen by avoiding those behaviors that you know will reduce such chances.

4. Small Talk/Big Talk

I cannot talk with a civet in the room.

—William Cowper (*Conversation*, 1782)

What do you say to a professor to begin an outwitting session? The answer is: just about anything you believe he or she might be interested in, although some kind of legitimate academic business is always appropriate. Just remember that there are two basic categories of Talk that apply to human interactions in general: Small and Big. For profs, you'll need both, but you'll also need to use them wisely and appropriately.

There is also a third category of Talk that is neither Big nor Small, but is unique to school and is heard so often that profs expect it from students, and that is Grade Talk. Grade Talk can always be used to start a conversation in a prof's office, and in fact it's an excellent excuse to go to that office the first time. But once you've used Grade Talk then your outwitting homework, including the OP, needs to drive your actions.

Grade Talk also gets old very quickly, and profs can easily form a negative opinion of someone who constantly worries about a few points on tests; that is especially true if you're already making an A (yes, it happens, a *lot*). If you see your prof in a bar (chapter 8), then a Small Talk starter is recommended (see below). Complimenting this prof on his or her course is always, and I do mean *always*, effecttive, but you'll need some kind of a lead-in to get to that point. Encounters somewhere between the extremes—office vs. bar—require a few adjustments of the Small/Big/Grade ratios, but these adjustments are pretty easy to learn from experience.

With respect to both Big and Small Talk, remember the old saying, usually attributed to Admiral Hyman Rickover, that "great minds talk about ideas, middle-sized minds talk about things, and small minds talk about other people." This saying is pretty true, so if you're going to talk about people, then do it in a "great mind" way. For example, "that was a great question _____ asked. Did you finish the answer, or was there something more?" People talk that is sure to cause you problems, and negate much of your outwitting investment, is the question: "how come _____ got credit for this question when I didn't, even though we studied together and our answers were exactly the same?"

Your prof could probably say "but your answers were not the same" but he or she won't. Instead, you'll probably get an explanation of why your answer was inadequate. This explanation is likely to be longer and more involved than you want it to be, especially because you're not going to get credit anyway. What you will accomplish is teaching your prof that you're a person who worries about why other students get credit, and that's not something you want your prof to learn. You want profs to learn that you are a person who worries about your own performance and doesn't care much what other people do on tests and assignments.

Back to talk. Nowadays, many students who need to be actively outwitting their profs are simply too shy for the job. You can't be shy, folks; you can't be afraid of profs or

[38]

have so much respect for them that you are reluctant to involve them in your journey toward success in life. See also Nicole Searcey's advice to her young relatives in chapter 12; Nicole was a champion outwitter, thus the invitation to contribute that chapter to this edition of OCP. One of her most valuable comments to her niece and nephews, classes of 2029, 2031, and 2033 respectively, regards such fear. Her advice? "Get over it!" (or words to that effect).

Shyness is sometimes natural, sometimes learned, or sometimes pounded into children, but in any case, it needs to be reduced, eliminated, or conquered. It's not in your best interests to be shy around profs mainly because shy students provide little or no feedback on how well a prof is doing his or her job. Generally profs want you to be assertive instead of afraid of them. So what you might need to get beyond the fear is a few conversation starters. Here are some specific examples that will work most if not all of the time:

Conversation starters:

These starters are listed in order from Small to Big, with typical and appropriate places to start them.

1. Hi. (Okay to use anywhere, any time; goes best with a smile or at least a nod.)

2. Hi. How's your day going? (Okay to use anywhere, any time.)

3. Hi. How's your semester going? (Okay to use anywhere, any time, especially if you've not seen this person since a previous semester.)

4. Hi. How's your semester going? Are you still teaching ____? (Okay to use anywhere, any time, especially if you've not seen this person since a previous semester and you did well in his/her class.)

5. Hi, Dr. _____. How's your day going? Hey, did you see that article in the paper [piece on TV, etc.] this morning about _____? (This one works best if you've used 1-3 above any time in the recent past, the prof knew who you were when you took his/her class, and you see this prof about once a week.)

6. Hi, Dr. _____. I was planning on coming by your office some time in the next couple of days . . . (This one requires a legitimate reason for going by the prof's office, and always works best if you've used 1-5 above.)

You may be thinking "how dumb can this guy be that he thinks I need to be told to say 'hi' to a college professor?" Well, I can be pretty dumb, but I also tend to view the world in terms of numbers, so that when I recognize students every day walking around campus, and they either turn away or look down when they see me, or perhaps feign talking so intently on their phones that they don't notice me then I realize these students are probably the tip of a large iceberg of people who could easily be outwitting a college prof but are either too shy, or too afraid, to do the first simple task, which is to say "hi." I'm not sure college students are ever told explicitly by people they seem to pay attention to (such as advisers) that it's okay to say "hi" to a prof. Nevertheless, saying "hi" is not only okay, it's also an essential part of any overall outwitting scheme.

Once you've made it through the above list, you should be over your shyness and well on your way to engaging any prof in a conversation provided the opportunity is available and appropriate. Some of you are going to read the above list and say to yourself: does this guy (JJJr) think I'm some kind of a born yesterday social deviant who can't say "hi" to a prof on campus if I want to (which is not always the case)? On the other hand, I know from experience that some of you are quaking in your boots at the thought of saying "hi" to a prof, and will continue to be regardless of what book you might have picked up including this one, especially (*especially!*) if you're in the company of some cool friends who disapprove mightily of your speaking to a college professor.

In this case your friends are not really all that cool. They're simply working overtime to stay below you on the scale of outwitting skills and their transcripts are likely to reflect their disdain for the tricks provided in this small book, that is, the tricks students used so successfully on me for forty-plus years. You, on the other hand, no matter how shy and reluctant you may be at the moment, are well on your way to becoming a sophisticated and polished college student with better grades than your friends, an excellent education to go with the grades, and great recommendations from your teachers. And what will eventually separate you from your not-so-cool friends is Big Talk.

Big Talk:

Big Talk is about ideas and concepts (see above quote from Hyman Rickover). Again, in my experience, a whole lot of college students rarely think about ideas and concepts, and instead spend a great deal of their time worrying about facts or about their ability to solve specific problems (chemistry, physics, math). Profs, however, live in a world of concepts and ideas. You don't have to live in this world, but it is to your decided benefit to be able to enter it at will.

In the past, when I've asked students for ideas and concepts, or given assignments that involved concepts, their response has typically been one of bewilderment. So for those of you who need some help, here is a list of ideas, expressed as assertions (some testable, others not) that are sure to stimulate some Big Talk. But be forewarned: Big Talk about ideas usually stirs up passions.

1. There is no God.

2. All organisms, including humans, evolve.

3. Liberal professors pollute young minds.

4. Women are not as smart as men in math and science.

5. Wealth accumulating in a small fraction of any population will benefit all members of that population.

6. Global health is of military importance to powerful nations.

7. Homosexuality is a sin.

8. Hollywood is responsible for the decline in American morals.

9. Climate change will destroy the United States faster than any terrorist groups can accomplish the same goal.

10. Abortion can be eliminated just by abstinence education in middle schools.

Obviously this list could go on for pages. And just as obviously, it was constructed for the sole purpose of stimulating your passions. If you need some more, and less volatile, ideas for use in conversations, you can always check around on the Internet. But you can certainly see from the above list how ideas can be powerful tools for engaging human beings in conversations, sometimes heated ones. In general, profs like heated conversations, but they also like people who are capable of engaging in such conversations without generating or feeling personal animosity.

Another trick that students have used on me, and one that involves Big Talk, is to ask for personal help on writing, usually by bringing in one of their papers for critique. The fact that I'm a biology professor instead of in the English Department probably validates this trick as outwitting, mainly because English profs usually are expected to provide such service. Nevertheless, it works.

[42]

Fairly extended conversations about sentence and paragraph structure, style, usage, clarity, and "what you are trying to accomplish with this piece" are usually relatively intimate ones, intellectually speaking, mainly because writing is, or at least can be, such a personal act. English profs engage in so much of this kind of talk that they are relatively immune to being outwitted by it, and indeed they may expect such personal interactions from students. Other profs, however, rarely have such conversations with students about their creative efforts. Art and music profs may be an exception, but you rarely have to outwit them; you just have to be a good artist or musician. So feel free to work your wiles on science, history, sociology, and economics profs who have asked you to write papers.

Just to validate the above points, I should tell you about a student from my BIOS 101 class (~230 students) in the fall of 2008. We did extemporaneous writings every Friday afternoon in class for fifteen minutes then followed that up with a typed version and a page of self-assessment every week for fourteen weeks. This student came by my office one day in the middle of the semester and wanted to talk about the dangerous types mentioned in the chapter "Advanced Outwitting."

We talked a little bit about difficult types then she pulled out her Friday writings to talk about how to improve. In other words, she was doing exactly what is recommended in the paragraph above. As a result of that interaction, I e-mailed her the next semester with an offer to be a reader on an unpublished book manuscript that eventually became *Pieces of the Plains: Memories and Predictions from the Heart of America* (2009). Her reading and comments were of substantial importance to the finishing of the book. The student's outwitting efforts paid off big time; she's acknowledged gratefully in *Pieces* and has an excellent letter of recommendation waiting for her when she needs it.

[43]

I should also probably tell you about my Friday afternoons at the University of Nebraska. Faculty members routinely adjourn to some local watering hole on Friday afternoons, sometimes in the company of their graduate students, for some beer and *really* heavy academic conversation. I've been known to do that, too, especially with doctoral students and post-docs who are pretty much the equivalent of faculty members. However, usually there are several undergraduates, both men and women, who do research in my lab. Often these students are doing honors theses, but not always. They vary from first year students to seniors.

At one of these particularly stimulating Friday afternoon sessions, I raised the question: How do we get the undergraduates involved in these kinds of conversations? After all, no male prof who values his job invites underage females to join him in a local bar, even though those coeds are extraordinarily intelligent and would make significant contributions to the Big Talk that occurs there. A young man named Ben Hanelt who was a doctoral student in my lab at the time suggested that we go down to a local coffee house at 3:30 on Fridays. The underage students would feel comfortable and welcome, and after an hour or so those who wished to head on down to Barry's Tavern could do it with a clear conscience. Thus began Friday Afternoon Coffee.

I've related this story before (Janovy, 2003; *Teaching in Eden*), but it's worth repeating. Friday Afternoon Coffee became an institution in my laboratory, and quite frankly, the Big Talk that occurred there often surpassed in quality that taking place later at Barry's. What did we talk about at Friday Afternoon Coffee? You name it, we talked about it. All professionalism issues, teaching strategies, research design, data analysis, ideas worth pursuing, current events, religion, politics, evolution, harassment in the workplace, etc.

I'm convinced those Friday Coffee conversations had a major impact on these students' ability to deal with workplace issues that will arise long after they have left the university, issues that I know will come up because I've seen it happen repeatedly. A few years ago my department tried to duplicate Friday Coffee by starting a course in professsionalism, required of all graduate students. One of the first things you learn as a young prof is that anything you say in class is in the public domain, especially in the electronic age. Facebook comments suggested our formal course was a complete failure. There is a difference between learning that results when students are *told* (required) to listen to some prof and the life-long learning that is acquired when students *choose* to have Big Talk conversations on a regular basis.

I have not seen faculty members sitting around at coffee talking with students, at least at my institution, since the Vietnam War days. In my humble opinion, when faculty and students don't spend at least some time sitting around talking Big Talk, something's obviously missing from the American higher education enterprise. Enough of the soap box. Do you want an ultimate outwitting weapon? Get together with a couple of your like-minded friends and invite a prof to coffee once a week for an entire school year and see what happens.

Final take-home message:

In general, college professors are people who love to talk, especially about ideas and concepts. If you can find a way to engage your profs in meaningful conversations then you have found a powerful outwitting device. But you can't be shy. Regardless of how reluctant you may be to actually have an extended conversation with some college

[45]

professor, remember that most of them appreciate your efforts in this regard and in the end these efforts will pay off with better recommendation letters and a higher quality education.

$$\frac{(ad - bc)^2}{(cz + d)^4} \cdot \frac{A'\left(\dfrac{az + b}{cz + d}\right)^2 + B'\left(\dfrac{az + b}{cz + d}\right) + C'}{\left(\dfrac{az + b}{cz + d}\right)^2 \left[1 - \dfrac{az + b}{cz + d}\right]^2} = \frac{Az^2 + Bz + C}{4z^2(1 - z)^2}$$

5. Tests and Grades

*. . . so that when the hour of dire need draws nigh,
it may find you not unnerved and untrained to stand
the test.*

—William James, *The Principles of Psychology* (1890)

There is no real way to outwit any college professor on tests, quizzes, and exams. You simply have to know e-nough about the course material to answer the questions or do the problems. So the question to be addressed in this chapter is not so much "how do I outwit a prof in order to make a good grade on an exam?" as it is "how do I make the prof believe that I've really studied the material and understand it far better than my test grades seem to indicate?"

The answer to the first of these questions, as I've said, is "you can't;" the answer to the second question is "it's possible, but you may not want to do it, especially if you're determined to make a bad grade in a class." Sorry, folks; tests are one area in which your ability to outwit a prof is severely constrained. But take heart; there's a slight chance of partial success. And, in general, students always (or at least usually) want to improve their record. So this chapter may be worth reading after all.

[47]

The simple cases:

What is a simple case? These individuals are ones who make good grades without a whole lot of effort, handling several kinds of tests—including multiple-choice, short answer essay, long essays, and math, chemistry, or physics problems—with relative ease. Simple cases also tend to have nice handwriting (easy for profs to read) and strong command of the English language (or in whatever language the course happens to be taught).

If you're a simple case then it's probably not worth your time to mess with this chapter, although I'd be flattered if you actually read it, give some thought to those things that might help your less simple-case peers, and pass your ideas along for a future edition. Don't worry about giving someone else some help, even if that help seems to be undeserved. Everyone is indeed better off when living in a reasonably well-educated nation, and any small amount of time you donate to this cause is time well spent.

If you are a simple case (and students typically recognize this trait in themselves fairly quickly) but are not making the grades you want to make, or impressing profs in a way that will get them to open doors for you later on, then you already know what the problem is, namely, that you just are not applying your talents to the tasks at hand. Here we're talking more about will than about ability. I'm not going to lecture you about applying your talents to the task; you have parents or legal guardians to do this job. I'll just reiterate what you already know: the record you assemble today is the vehicle you will ride into your near future.

Distant futures, for example 10 years or more, are not really very predictable, and it's entirely possible that you can get your act together and be king or queen of the world a decade hence. But if you want to get into medical school or law school three years from now, it's time to read this book carefully and start using the advice no matter how easy the coursework is at the time you're doing it. So go look in the mirror. If the person you see there is working below capacity—for whatever reason—but truly desires to be somewhere in the near future that depends quite a bit on working up to capacity then you need to have a talk with that kid in the mirror.

As a closer to this section, I'll say that the biggest danger to Simple Cases is the self-destructive behavior that occurs commonly on university campuses and tends to involve automobiles, alcohol, and sex with strangers, all in various combinations. I'm not trying to sound like your mother on purpose; I'm just stating a fact of college life.

The more difficult cases:

Let's assume you consider yourself a "more difficult case;" that is, you struggle a little bit with exams and sincerely believe that your grades are not a true reflection of either your ability or what you've learned in class. Maybe I can be of help, if for no other reason than having dealt with literally thousands of people exactly like you. Again, unfortunately, the cure is going to sound more like "being a good student" than like "outwitting college professors."

I understand it's far more fun to outwit someone than to knuckle down and solve problems. That's why I use the term "unfortunately." I wish it were all fun—smoke and mirrors type fun, fooling a guy in a position of power type fun—to become a better test performer. It's not. So if you're not ready for this advice, go on to some more fun parts of this book. But if you're ready, here's true and correct advice from an insider (= one who makes out your exams and grades your work), starting with the easiest one on which to make progress:

The essay test (either long or short answer):

(1) Work on your penmanship. Practice writing legibly. *You* may be perfectly capable of reading your own handwriting, but that remarkable skill doesn't mean that anyone else can read it. Poor handwriting is probably the source of more lost points on essay exams than any other factor. Profs just get sick and tired of trying to decipher scrawl. Often, however, if you've answered the first question well, they'll skip through the later scrawl and give you the benefit of the doubt. But don't count on this lucky event happening; the first question might be the one you know least about, and in that case, the scrawl-skipping will work to your distinct disadvantage.

As a rule of thumb, some perfect stranger should be able to read your handwriting as easily as he or she reads a printed page. Always (always!) use dark ink—black or dark blue—or if a pencil is required, a dark and sharpened lead. Your letters should be large enough to read at arm's length. Never trust a college prof to have eagle-eye vision (or an owl's hearing, either), especially if he or she is over the age of 50.

(2) Work on your grammar. Whatever you do, do not make any of the truly common mistakes made by college students (see also the next chapter on papers). The truly common mistakes are:

a. Using "it's" when you actually mean "its" or vice versa.

b. Using "alot" when you actually mean "a lot".

c. Using "there" when you actually mean "their" or vice versa.

d. Using the wrong verb form. If you were born in the United States, for example, there is no excuse for using "went" when you mean "gone" either in writing or in speech.

e. Using the incorrect possessive form of any word, for example "cars" when you actually mean "car's."

This list could be much longer, but I believe you get the drift. Poor grammar will hurt you not only on the next exam, but also on the next job interview, the next potential promotion, and the next time you have to accomplish some real business in the real world, whatever that business might be, including contracts, agreements involving money, pre-nuptial agreements, divorce proceedings, complaints to a school board about how your child is being taught, you name it. Use correct grammar. Alternatively, change your name to one that sounds exceedingly foreign so that the person reading your writing believes that English is your second language and you've just started learning it. Then you'll be admired instead of ridiculed.

(3) Practice writing in complete sentences. Failure to write in complete sentences is probably the second most common source of lost points on essay exams mainly because such failure suggests to a grader that you are not well educated and thus don't know much about anything, including the subject over which you're being tested. You may also have been told to write in complete sentences, so read the directions and follow them before you start your essay. If you can easily generate sentences that are grammatically correct and at least 15 words long then you have taken a major step toward getting better grades on all essay exams no matter what the subject.

(4) Practice writing short paragraphs in which there is both an idea and a fact to support the idea. This essay technique is usually difficult for students to learn, but it's the technique that profs use all the time in their own work.

So if you can master it, you've made some major progress toward actually getting better grades, especially if you combine this technique with the above advice. Beyond these four behaviors, only true knowledge and understanding of the subject matter stands between you and better grades. Now for the most difficult of all exams:

The multiple-choice test:

(1) Remember why profs give multiple-choice tests. These exams are easy to grade, so if you're in a large class, chances are you're in for a large number of multiple-choice questions. If you walk into a large lecture hall the first day of class, you can almost be assured that your exams will be multiple-choice or some version of it, using a bubble sheet for the answers.

Remember also that these exams can be a real pain in the neck to make out, so your prof is probably not particularly happy about the exam either, except to the extent that he or she doesn't have to prepare a show just to keep you entertained and hopefully make you educated for 50 minutes. So the main objective is ease of grading and not necessarily evaluating your knowledge or understanding.

A second objective of multiple-choice tests is to separate students into groups based on performance. That is, profs need written evidence to support their decision to award some grade. This second objective has little or nothing to do with your learning, but everything to do with your formal record in college.

(2) Remember that multiple-choice tests are actually more exercises in reading than in whatever subject the class concerns. Students tend to forget this principle, and as a result, end up losing points unnecessarily. So whatever course you're taking, study it the same way you would a foreign language first then deal with the subject matter

itself. That is, you have to know the words in order to understand the language. To illustrate this point, here are a couple of multiple-choice questions from one of my recent exams. The subject is embryological development.

1. In Protostomia, you would expect (a) the blastopore to become the anus (b) the anus to become the blastopore (c) the mouth to become the blastopore (d) the blastopore to become the mouth (e) the mouth to develop from mesoderm.

2. In radially cleaving embryos (a) fate of blastomeres is established in the first cell division (b) the fate of the blastopore is established by the 4-cell stage (c) the fate of blastomeres is not determined until at least after the first few cell divisions (d) the archenteron develops from mesoderm (e) none of these.

Now, here are the same questions but with the vocabulary words (= the foreign language of biology) replaced with gibberish:

1. In wnitlnlcy, you would expect (a) the xclapic to become the ipxhp (b) the nmnm to become the xclapic (c) the trtrtz to become the xclapic (d) the xclapic to become the trtrtz (e) the trtrtz to ghjklnm from cvbzoupwty.

2. In prritzx rucbwyx eicvbasms (a) the ewrt of hklwuciths is plknytxcvb in the first pgksl rycbnqtzx (b) the ewrt of the xclapic is plknytxcvb by the 4-pgksl wtxvnqm (c) the ewrt of hklwuciths is not etdsytpmlk until at least after the first few pgksl rycbnqtzxs (d) the tcbnsxuiqb ghjklnms from cvbzoupwty (e) none of these.

Obviously there is no way you're going to be able to answer such questions, or even to guess intelligently, until you learn what those words mean and can use them in sentences in the same manner as does the writer of such questions.

There will be some classes in which multiple-choice questions actually require that you solve a problem of some other kind in order to find the correct answer. Chemistry and physics courses are notorious for these kinds of questions. Depending on how long the exam is, such tests, and multiple-choice tests in general, may place a real premium on the speed with which you work, regardless of your intelligence or preparation. This premium on speed is especially evident in large classes.

(3) Remember that multiple-choice questions usually are simply complete sentences that are either true or false. In the above examples all you have to do is look at the introductory phrase and the answers to realize that each of the five answers, when combined with the introducetory phrase, makes a complete sentence. Then all you have to decide is whether each complete sentence is true or false (typically easier said than done). When introductory phrase + answer make a false sentence that fact is usually revealed by a key word or two.

(4) Key words are the big key to answering multiple-choice questions. In the first of the above questions, "Protostomia" is the key word because the very definition of that term is choice (a). In the second of those questions, "radially" and "fate" are the two key words, leading immediately to choice (c). Even though the subject is biology in this case, the principles apply to almost every course in which multiple-choice questions are given on exams. If you visit your prof after performing poorly on a multiple-choice exam, chances are that he or she will pull out a copy of the exam and start through a few questions, circling key words in the process. Looking for key words is a way of learning to read such exams the same way your prof does.

(5) Try not to change correct answers to incorrect ones. Every time I get a bubble sheet back from the graders, I

see questions that students have changed from right to wrong. I'm not really sure why this change happens, but when I talk to these students, it seems like they're trying to outguess me instead of dealing with the question itself. So my advice is to always read the question literally, and not guess what the prof might or might not have intended.

Only the most bored and sadistic profs try to devise trick questions or demand that you read their minds in order to answer correctly. The vast majority of profs are busy as hell, irritated because they have to make out an exam, and eager to get the test over so they can get back to this major ego trip called "lecturing." So they're not likely to waste time trying to make questions ambiguous and obscure psychic exercises, at least on purpose; most of them, however, are quite capable of writing such questions by accident or out of self-delusion, thinking they are perfectly clear.

(6) *If you're allowed to comment on questions, and if you're unsure about a particular answer or feel like a question is not a good one then always (__always!__) make the comment in writing, using the phrase "I answered question ____ with choice ____ because . . ."* In most cases, you'll get the question correct anyway; thinking through your reasons helps you with the rationale for choosing between options.

(7) *Make sure you answer all the questions.* Again, this is a very simple rule, although some profs are very devious and try to design multiple-choice tests that either penalize you for guessing or give you choices that specify two or more other choices. My advice is to avoid these profs if at all possible.

(8) *Always, **ALWAYS**, keep your exams if allowed to, record the correct answers, and use these old exams to*

[55]

study for the final. You'd be surprised at how many students ignore this obvious rule. Profs can be quite lazy and therefore use some of the same questions over and over again. I've often used the same test questions multiple times and even given students the questions in advance. Statistically, this behavior on my part makes little or no difference in class averages because so many students ignore my advice to study the questions before the test.

Fill in the blanks:

These kinds of tests are a major pain in the neck for both students, who often struggle for exactly the right answer, and profs who want to grade them quickly and are frustrated by poor writing. Fill in the blanks questions put a real premium on penmanship mainly because of this desire—on the part of the prof—to grade the papers in the least amount of time, and sometimes while doing something else like drinking wine, talking to his or her spouse, watching TV, or playing with a pet. My best advice in this case is to work on your penmanship and read the book or your notes often enough so that you recognize sentences lifted directly out of a text or handout. If the prof uses such sentences, and simply takes out a word then you're in business.

Label a diagram:

Students think they like these kinds of test questions, but remember that the prof has all the trump cards in this particular game. He or she can give you diagrams that tend to require more detailed knowledge than students expect, or ask for interpretations to accompany labels. You can also get diagrams that are based on the course material but may not have actually been presented either in lecture or in the textbooks. Any prof who gives you a diagram straight out of the text and asks only for labels is a very lazy prof;

in this case your good grade does not indicate much of an education received.

If you believe you may be asked to label diagrams then practice your visual literacy along with whatever other studying you may be doing for this particular exam. By "visual literacy" I mean the ability to convert words into pictures and vice versa. Write a sentence then draw a picture that "says" the same thing; similarly, draw a picture that conveys the same ideas as a sentence in your text. This is a skill area that will serve you well in any number of settings, especially after college, but if you're expecting a diagram quiz then practicing your visual literacy will make your study much more effective than it would be otherwise. After all, that's what your textbook authors do when they assemble a book for which you and millions of other students across the country pay $200 or more.

Some final and overall general rules:

(1) Make sure you actually answer the question that is asked. You'd be very surprised to discover how often violation of this elementary rule costs students points on exams. Trust me; it happens a lot (in fact, *a whole lot*). This rule doesn't apply so much to math, chemistry, and physics classes where the problems are fairly obvious ones, but in the earth and biological sciences, and humanities, be sure you read the question carefully and make sure you answer it and not one that you just happened to have studied.

(2) Make sure you obey the test instructions. I mark off a lot (a whole lot!) of points for violation of this simple rule. If a short answer essay exam asks for complete sentences, write complete sentences (subject, verb, object).

(3) Always (always!) *visit with your prof individually if you do not score as well on the exam as you'd like to.* This simple rule is violated *en mass* by literally hundreds of

thousands of college students every day. When you visit, ask why you missed points and how to improve your performance, even if the answers to those questions are obvious to you. Your level of responsibility will positively impress your prof. This impression might make a difference in your grade or it might not, but it certainly will not hurt your overall record in college.

Grades:

Pay attention to the grading system and criteria in every class. Profs are generally required to spell out their grading policies in the syllabus; if they don't then they're just asking for a problem of some kind, often a formal appeal. In any case, keep all your graded material, and I do mean *ALL OF IT!* Every quiz, every exam, every piece of paper that has a mark on it. If your prof posts grades electronically, be sure to copy and paste, or print out, every entry into your line on the spreadsheet. Keep all this evidence until you are convinced you were graded fairly.

Most university departments have grade appeals committees, or at least should. I was on ours for several years and read a number of such appeals. In general, grades are changed by committees for only one reason: there is tangible evidence that a student was not graded in accordance with stated policies. Thus it is very important to save all your work as well as any statements about grading that are in the syllabus.

Final take-home message:

When dealing with exams, you're not going to beat the system very often or very much, but it is entirely possible to maximize your performance on exams, especially over the course of a year. Just remember that this advice is not a quick fix, but a recommended set of behaviors that maximize, at least from a statistical point of view, student performance on tests. **And, always keep all your graded materials, all of them, until you're sure you were graded fairly!**

6. Papers

Fire in each eye, and papers in each hand,

They rave, recite, and madden round the

Land.

> —Alexander Pope (*Epistle to Dr. Arbuthnot*, 1734)

Students write papers, period. Depending on where you end up going to college, you may write a whole lot of papers. The first thing to remember about a paper is that for the student, it's often a massive job, especially if done legitimately (more on this subject below), but for profs, papers are documents that take up a bunch of the profs' time, time they would rather be spending writing their own papers. So paper assignments can be quite unpleasant at both ends—the writing (student) and the reading (prof).

Any activity that is assumed to be unpleasant by all participants is an opportunity simply asking for some outwitting behavior, especially when one of the participants is in the power position. Papers therefore offer one of the most effective and powerful devices for outwitting your prof. All you have to do is think of this as a game, one that is set up for you to win. In fact, this is a game that your prof is just begging you to win.

If your classmates don't have a copy of this book then the advice you'll pick up in the next few pages will make you stand out from your peers in a very positive way. But there is one matter that we have to agree upon right up front before I tell you how to outwit people like me, at least as far as papers are concerned. We need to agree that my advice is going to sound reasonably serious. Some of you may even be suspicious that it's "teacherly" advice, in the sense that I'm telling you to do what profs want you to do in order to get a good college education. Well, that may be the case, but the advice is still good. In fact, the more your classmates ignore the obvious, the easier it is to outwit your prof and make you look like a million dollars in his or her eyes.

Therefore, I suggest that as you read this chapter, you maintain the outwitting mentality. You're not following my suggestions because they will turn you into a good college student and a well educated individual (which they are likely to do by default). You're following them because your prof is frustrated as hell with all those students who can't seem to remember that books are printed on paper and that the word "Internet" is a synonym for "shallow convenience."

I'll quickly dispose of my opinions about the Internet; then we can get down to the serious matter of converting you from a B student into an A student. First, the Internet is here to stay, at least until the end of the civilized world. It's now as much a part of human biology as toenails, hair, and sex, so needs to be accepted as such. Second, there are a whole lot of truly great things to be said about the Internet, and some of the information on it is quite valid, or at least close to being valid, e.g., airline schedules. Third, Google is one of the most remarkable innovations of all human history. In fact, Google is such a powerful inno-

[62]

vation that the word "Google" has become a verb in the vernacular in addition to its role as a proper noun.

Finally, and this is my most important comment, the Internet usually *teaches* expedience and shallowness, especially expedience, but your prof wants you to *learn* discipline and to explore subjects in depth. Your prof has this desire because he or she knows that discipline and depth are acquired traits that will carry you far in life, whereas expedience and shallowness will always get you in trouble and bring you discouragement out there in the real world. You wouldn't be particularly enamored of a significant other who was shallow and expedient, so why should you tolerate these traits in a boss or employee? You shouldn't, and most of you won't. So we need to get beyond the Internet.

Getting beyond the Internet:

In college, there are generally two kinds of assigned papers, (1) those in which the prof actually tolerates, asks for, or even requires, you to use the Internet as a resource, and then (2) all the others. I'll deal with (2), all the others, first. The reason I'm dealing with all the others first is because they cause profs the most frustration. That frustration stems not only from student behavior, but also from things over which students have no control, for example slashed library budgets, lost books, and cancelled journal subscriptions.

Let's assume the worst, namely that your prof has required you to use resources other than Wikipedia. In other words, you can't, or at least are not supposed to, simply go to Google, do a quick search on your key word then copy text from some online page and paste the material into your paper. The first step in outwitting this prof is to ask specifically what sources are allowed. I'm guessing you will be the only student in class who actually asks for this infor-

[63]

mation then pays attention to the prof when he or she answers your question.

So either raise your hand to ask what sources are allowed, or better yet, go to that prof's office, or, as a last resort, e-mail the prof with the same question. E-mail is the last resort because you want this prof to see you in person, see your curious, attentive, expression as you ask a serious question to which your classmates are oblivious.

The next piece of advice is so straightforward I'm almost embarrassed to tell you about it, and wouldn't even mention it if I had not had literally hundreds, maybe thousands, of college students totally ignore information delivered directly into their faces. So here is the advice I'm embarrassed to tell you: *when your prof takes the time to answer this question about allowed sources then follow that prof's suggestions to the letter.*

As a minimum, try that prof's advice and help before seeking additional help, so that you can at least tell this person you've tried to find the right sources. From your real efforts you'll have enough original experience to make those efforts sound legitimate. At this point, you're probably already noticing a difference between your classmates and yourself. Your classmates probably are still hitting on Google and copying and pasting text that any half-witted prof can recognize instantly for what it is, namely, shallow, plagiarized, and expedient.

What are some of these non-Internet "right" sources? They range from newspaper reports and magazine stories, to serious scholarly books (= monographs), to original journal articles. These sources vary significantly in terms of their underlying accuracy, but journal articles are at least reviewed anonymously, usually. Scholarly journal articles are often called "primary literature" because they typically contain detailed methods of research, actual data, statistical analysis, and a professional scholar's interpretation of the data. Profs love students who are able to deal with the primary literature, regardless of the subject.

I apologize for the fact that learning to recognize primary literature is the first step toward actually becoming a better scholar. I'd prefer to keep this discussion going in terms of outwitting someone, inspiring this prof to give you a higher grade than you deserve to get. Unfortunately, just by trying to outwit the prof, you might well end up actually deserving the better grade. Again, I apologize for this problem. Certain things are inextricably linked, such as, in this case, outwitting someone and actually learning something by doing it. Back to the subject of primary literature.

You have access to primary literature from two places: your institution's library and some full text online sites. The number of electronic full text resources is increasing, and using them is generally not the same as googling a subject then cutting and pasting from somebody's web page. By "full text" I mean a real journal article, just as it appeared in the paper version, but available online. Sometimes you get actual full text articles by doing a Google search, but not very often. In general, your library has to subscribe to an electronic full text service before you can easily get this kind of material, or much of a diversity of it, and these subscriptions can cost several thousand dollars a year. I suggest you go to the library, actually handle some real paper issues of journals in your major, and learn what a full primary literature article looks like so you can recognize one when you see it on the web.

If you use one of these sources, be sure to have the entire article in your possession—from title page through the bibliography—either as a paper printout or as a file. Routinely I ask students to see the articles they're using as sources. When a student is able to instantly produce photocopies or full text printouts, especially with sections highlighted, then that student has made a major positive impression. In fact, the first time you actually photocopy a journal article or print out a full text primary source and read it carefully, using a highlighter, you've acquired a transferable skill that will serve you well no matter what the course.

If your library subscribes to full text sources then obtaining these primary literature papers is not the same as getting them off a Google search. Instead, getting such papers is the equivalent of finding them in the published journal and making a photocopy. The only difference—and it's a reasonably important one—is that you don't end up spending quiet and reflective time by yourself back in the library stacks surrounded by real books printed on acid-free paper. Instead, you might well have obtained this scholarly publication at three in the morning with your iPod stuck into your ears blasting some Pissing Razors heavy metal into your frontal lobes. There is a real difference between the two experiences, and this difference is not only in the convenience of obtaining primary literature when the library is closed. Try the real library once or twice and you'll see what I mean.

Now that you've mastered the primary literature trick, here's one for advanced outwitting: if you can find out how your prof highlights sections of photocopied papers, and do yours the same way then you've stepped up a notch in this prof's eyes. If you see him or her using a copy of something with a lot of pencil marks on it, use a pencil on yours. If he or she uses a yellow highlighter then use a yellow highlighter yourself. But make sure this prof actually sees your photocopy with your marks on it. A visit to his or her office with a cooked-up question is a good way to accomplish this task.

Caving in to the Internet:

The first and absolutely non-negotiable rule for use of the Internet is: if you use Internet sources, always document them carefully and evaluate them critically, even if not required to do so. And cite your URL sources for *everything*. **_Everything_**. Be totally candid about and completely up front and open with whatever you get off the web. We are assuming that your prof either allows or requires Internet sources. The outwitting trick is subtle but important and effective: make sure your prof can easily distinguish between what you've taken off the Internet and what you've done all by yourself.

In order to perform this trick you need to read carefully what your prof has actually asked you to do. This advice seems rather obvious, but at least 60% of my students in the beginning courses either don't read the assignment or don't do it. *So do what you've been asked to do.* The fact that so many of your classmates won't actually do the assignment means that just by doing it, you're outwitting your prof a little bit. That is, you're doing something unexpected and getting him or her to react positively toward such behavior.

Your college library may have its own web pages, and somewhere on those pages may be advice for evaluating Internet sources and for citing them in your papers, or listing them in your bibliographies if used. Again, the outwitting trick is pretty simple: *follow the advice*. Many of your classmates are not going to follow it, and if you do then immediately you've created a positive impression. The one thing I cannot tell you exactly how to do is actually demonstrate that you've done what the library staff advises you to do in order to evaluate Internet sources. You'll have to figure out the phraseology for your own paper. But if there are examples provided by the library staff, make your paper read exactly, *exactly*, like those examples.

Physical appearance:

The physical appearance of your paper is important. The trick here is to make it look as close as you can to the kind of thing your prof has to write for his or her own scholarly work. All profs must obey certain rules for preparing their manuscripts, and usually those rules are written in the journals (primary literature) to which they submit papers. On the other hand, professors' papers are not always written in a format that is common, or even looks like most students think a paper should look. So the outwitting trick is to get close to something that looks familiar to a prof, but without necessarily having to follow his or her scholarly journal's editorial policies to the letter.

Here are some simple rules that if followed will make your paper look reasonably similar to whatever your prof is writing himself or herself. Like all rules in this book, these are subject to modification by your prof. But in the absence of very specific instructions about format, these rules will produce a paper that's at least visually pleasing. I've provided them as a checklist just to make them easier to follow.

_____ Headers and footers: Avoid them, but if you must use them, make them a single word in a small font, with the page number incorporated.

_____ Your name: On every page.

_____ Page numbers: Use them, and place them on the bottom right of the sheet unless told otherwise.

_____ Fonts: 12 point Times New Roman, period. Italics are okay in special cases, e.g. scientific names (genus and species only), certain foreign words, and an occasional emphasis.

_____Printer ink: Black and dark.

_____Margins: One inch, although an inch and a quarter is okay on the left.

_____Right justification: Don't do it.

_____Line spacing: Double.

_____Paragraphs: Two to three a page (one and a half if you're an accomplished writer).

_____Bibliography: Essential, usually, especially in a research paper. If you are not given a style then pick one from the primary literature and use it habitually for everything.

_____Title page: Nice but usually not necessary.

_____Staple or paper clip: Staple at upper left unless informed otherwise.

_____Pictures: Nice if appropriate and in context, but never try to substitute a picture for text and always credit your picture sources.

_____Due date: Turn it in or ask for an extension a couple of days in advance. Be sure to have a valid reason if you ask for an extension (waiting for interlibrary loan, etc.).

_____Revisions: If allowed or requested, do them immediately and return the next draft in a timely manner.

_____Grade check: It's always a good idea to go through your paper with your prof after it is graded, especially if there are extensive comments on it. But be sure to deal with those comments before you ask for an explanation.

_____Final suck-up: Choose this activity carefully. Only you can judge whether this prof is the kind of person who is vulnerable to final suck-up outwitting, whether you

[69]

are interested enough in your own writing skills to carry it off, and whether trying it might actually help you in other classes. By final suck-up I mean asking a prof about subtle issues of style, sentence and paragraph structure, and narrative sequence. Not all profs will be able to respond to such questions, and some may be outright threatened by them, especially if these folks are not good writers themselves.

E-mail and text messages:

We all use e-mail, and if we don't then we're both extraordinarily liberated and extraordinarily out of touch with the reality of day-to-day life in the 21st Century, at least as that life is lived throughout much of the world. Text messages on your cell phone are a different issue, and one that can be dealt with very easily: quit. You'll be a better communicator in general within a couple of days.

Why will this remarkable transformation occur? The answer is simple: *text messaging trains you to habitually do all the wrong things in writing, and probably in general use of the language, period.* So if you'll simply quit participating in that training activity, your communication skills will begin growing immediately. Or at least they'll stop deteriorating. You'll also gain about two or three hours a day.

Alternatively, take the time and effort to make your text messages grammatically perfect, with real words, punctuation, etc. You'll be surprised what a positive impression that practice makes on older folks (like profs). This advice really works, trust me. If you persist in using a lot of text messages, making them all grammatically correct will start to pay off in terms of enhanced communication skills within a week. Furthermore, those skills will transfer to all your other writing assignments.

The e-mail rules are very simple, and in fact there is only one: Always (*always!*) use correct grammar in your e-mail messages, capitalizing any words that would normally be capitalized in a typical college textbook, inserting punctuation where it should be, using complete sentences, and checking your spelling. If you follow this rule, even when writing to your best friends, your communication skills will slowly improve over time. But if you're writing to a prof then follow this one simple rule you will immediately stand out from the crowd, and in a very positive way.

Why will you stand out? Again, the answer is simple: *because when using e-mail, so many of your friends act like they are totally oblivious to basic grammatical conventions and correct spelling.* Your prof notices grammar and spelling in every communication, no matter what the medium. That trait does not make him or her an ivory tower nerd. Instead, it's a characteristic he or she shares with successful people in the business community, people who will be interviewing you for a real job in a few short years and care more about your writing ability than your burger-flipping manual dexterity.

Some excessive outwitting advice:

This advice is well above and beyond what is necessary to outwit profs who assign papers, but I'm inclined to pass it along anyway just because some of you might be unusual students, not necessarily unusually *good* students, but just unusual in some ill-defined way. My final piece of advice is to practice writing, especially if you are at an institution in which profs tend to assign a lot of papers or give essay exams. Write about anything—personal letters, opinions, stuff just to get something off your chest but would never send. But write in complete sentences—subject, verb, object, and prepositional phrases. Something in one sentence needs to remind a reader of what has been said in the previous sentence. About two or three times a

[71]

page, your string of sentences ought to bring some idea to closure. Then you're ready to start a new paragraph.

Practice paragraphing, deciding when there is a natural break between sentences. The first sentence of one paragraph should remind a reader of what has been said in the previous paragraph, although each paragraph should be a piece of "stand alone" literature. In other words, if you lift that paragraph out of your paper and print it on a blank sheet then it should tell a small and complete story all by itself. This requirement means that the opening sentence needs to establish the subject of that paragraph, and the closing sentence ought to finish a short discussion of that subject. A reader who finishes the paragraph ought to think "that makes sense" and thus be prepared for your next idea or assertion.

The above two paragraphs are quite self-referential in the sense that they illustrate these writing techniques.

My closing piece of advice is to give some thought to how much of yourself you want to write into a paper. From a reader's (prof's) perspective, the ideal amount is some, and hopefully a recognizable fraction. Remember that this paper is just that—a paper—not some summary of your self image, some accounting sheet of net intellectual or e-motional worth, or a key to your soul. At least it need not be. If you are determined to turn in papers that fulfill those criteria, make sure they are in an English class instead of Physics, and make sure the assigned subject is something like "ME AND WHO I REALLY AM" and not "Analysis of the Character Role of Weaponry in Vietnam War Era A-merican Fiction."

On the other hand, your prof will be reading so much dry, formulaic, college student here's-what-I-believe-this-prof-wants type prose that a little bit of originality will make your paper stand out like your great grandmother at a hip-hop concert. It's okay to say things in your own phraseology. Just make sure you say them in a way that's grammatically correct and avoids slang.

Final take-home message:

Papers may be the most important product of your college career, and provide an excellent opportunity for you to acquire skills that will serve you well in the years after graduation. Students who treat papers as a throw-away pain in the neck are missing a terrific chance to improve their lives after college, mainly because people in general, including employees in all kinds of occupations, are simply terrible writers.

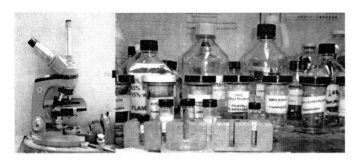

7. Projects

He had been eight years upon a project for extracting sunbeams out of cucumbers...

—Jonathan Swift

1726, *Voyage to Laputa*

Projects are without a doubt a more powerful device for outwitting a college professor than any other that is available to a student. The very nature of a "project" provides such power, and most profs readily acknowledge this attribute of the endeavor. Although a project is one of the most effective means of beating the system, the vast majority of students rarely if ever use one. If you're ready to become one of the privileged elite who work with a prof on some project, read on. But if you're reluctant to try this most effective outwitting trick then wait a year or two until you grow up a little bit and are not quite so afraid of college professors.

Why might you want to do independent study? The primary reason, for the purposes of this book, is that it's the most effective way to get the so-called "silver bullet" recommendation letter. Such a letter, from a faculty member, contains the phrase "I would trust [your name here] completely as [my family physician, my child's elementary school teacher, my accountant, my attorney, my . . . (your major)]."

These kinds of letters typically open a whole lot of doors. They are expensive, however, in terms of time and effort, and especially so if you don't really want to do independent study. The only other reason to do independent study is that you want to, and are personally interested enough in the subject to commit the time and effort. I don't want to discuss the latter possibility yet; it sounds too much like either an epiphany or serious student behavior.

Back to outwitting. In general, if you're even thinking about independent study then the most important rule in dealing with profs is *don't be afraid of them.* That command is easier for most students to say than to obey. Just remember that profs are people. They have bills to pay, spouses and significant others to spend time with, houses to maintain, and cars that have mechanical troubles, all in addition to favorite foods, favorite athletic teams, kids playing soccer, hobbies, and individual tastes in music. In other words, profs are about like your parents, and they're likely to be fairly good predictors of what you yourself will be like, socially, in a few years. They're probably a little more liberal than you are, and that's because they tend to read a lot, especially history. But in general, they're not very dangerous, and they're fairly receptive to meaningful communications from about anyone. "Meaningful" is the key word.

As a general rule, profs rate activities, including communication, on a meaningfulness scale that is displayed mostly against their personal scholarly interests. History profs, for example, typically consider reading and talking about history to be meaningful activities, but physics profs might well consider history to be quite subordinate to discussions about experimental equipment. You're not going to even think about a project, however, unless you're interested in the area yourself, and have decided to budget the time to pursue the independent work. So here is my first and most important rule about projects: *Don't consider doing one unless you really want to and can and will take enough time to do it well and bring it to closure.* This most powerful outwitting tool therefore comes with a price. If you're not ready, quit reading this chapter and go on to one that discusses some tricks you're more likely to use successfully.

Getting started:

Let's assume that you've made the decision to embark on a project with an as yet unchosen prof who will guide your work. What do you need to do in order to actually engage in independent, supervised, research (= a project)? The first thing to do, having gotten beyond the decision stage, is to talk to your fellow students. Ask them about their research experiences and analyze the responses carefully. Their mentors should be readily available for consultation, should help when asked, should tolerate mistakes early but correct those mistakes gently, always preserving a student's dignity, and should have student success as a personal goal.

This last characteristic is the most important. It should be in the vested interest of the prof for you to bring your project to closure and make him or her look good by doing so. These kinds of profs are begging to be outwitted and if you behave correctly, they will actually participate in the game as a player on your side.

The two key ingredients are time and an ability to set priorities. You must either have or take the time. I'm not speaking of a schedule, but of some flexible time that is scattered in two and three hour blocks. Ideally, for example, having two hours completely free in the afternoon, Monday, Wednesday, and Friday, is almost a prerequisite for independent study. Being able to set aside a four or five hour block of time twice a week is even better. Are you working two jobs just to stay in school? Are you a scholarship athlete? Are you an older non-traditional student with a couple of kids? Are you a senior officer in your Greek house? If the answers to these questions are "yes" then it's probably a good idea to go ahead and read this chapter, but with the realization that it may not have much in the way of advice for improving your academic record.

The priority part is easy. Can you keep your phone turned off for that length of time—six to ten hours a week? Can you stay away from the Internet for that period? Can you do without your iPod and music? Will your significant other leave you alone long enough to get your independent work done? Do you *like* the subject you're studying? Do you have the disturbing habit of spending a few hours completely alone doing some intellectual activity of your own choosing (reading non-assigned non-fiction books, visiting museums, writing anything but especially poetry or fiction, playing a musical instrument)? If the answers to all these questions are "yes," you're on the way to some silver bullet type behaviors.

The first big step:

The first thing to do is simply make an appointment with the chosen prof then ask if he or she advises students in independent study. That question will usually produce an answer not only to this question but also to several others, for example whether the prof is interested in you as a potential project advisee, whether there are other students also working on projects under his or her direction, and so forth. Often you can determine just from a prof's classroom behavior and demeanor whether he or she could be a good project adviser.

But profs also can be choosy about who they will advise on projects. Students often approach me and ask not so much whether they can work in my lab, but whether I have any advice for them, given the fact that they've expressed an interest in undergraduate research. In essence, they've allowed me to decide whether they are the kind of individual I want to recruit. I always suggest they contact a number of other faculty members who seem to do well with undergraduates. Sometimes the students end up working with others, but periodically they come back to my lab. The bottom line is that the student—you—must take the first big step of making the appointment, keeping it, and asking the question: can you help me get involved in undergraduate research?

What's likely to happen next:

After you've taken that first step successfully, and someone has agreed to accept you as an independent study advisee, what happens next? The answer to this question depends quite a bit on your area of study, but in general one of two things is likely to happen. Either you will start writing a research proposal, or you'll start working on the project. Eventually you'll do both, of course, but some profs want students to start digging into the literature and formulating their ideas—i.e., writing the proposal—before actually starting to work. Other profs want students to start working immediately so that the experience will help the student make sense of the literature.

Personally, because of the nature of our research, I fall into the latter category, but humanities and social science profs often want a student to do a literature review first. In either case, however, you'll eventually need to find a question to answer. The attempt to answer this question, the one burning in your brain, then becomes your project.

The most successful profs give their students at least a little bit of help finding an appropriate question. Such profs usually have a long list of appropriate questions hidden back in a file, and spend the first few weeks with an independent study student finding ways to convince the student that he or she has actually come up with the question by himself or herself. You need to understand that this kind of leading is simply an innocuous part of the game. But once you have your question, and have a sense of how to use the resources at your disposal to answer it (e.g., laboratory equipment and supplies in the sciences, good library or survey sources in the humanities and social sciences), you're in for the long haul.

The long haul:

A truly successful project typically requires at least a year, and often two. It's the long haul that allows you to earn the "silver bullet" letter of recommendation. It's your opportunity to demonstrate, again and again, your maturity, responsibility, insight, perceptiveness, and determination. Whatever you do, don't be put off by initial failure; indeed, how you respond to disappointment may be an important part of your growing maturity. Regardless of your particular project, however, you will need to gather data regularly, modify your study if dictated by initial observations, keep accurate records and files, grow in your technological skills, and most important—from the perspective of outwitting a prof—acquire the vocabulary of the discipline.

The words of a discipline are the key to becoming a legitimate member of the intellectual community in the eyes of most professors. So if you end up working on a project, by all means, decide in the beginning that you are going to learn the words that make you sound like a professional then practice using those words. Practice on your parents, your friends, about anyone who will listen, although sometimes dates are not very receptive to such practice, and in a few cases will be turned off rather quickly by arcane vocabulary, especially in the sciences. But let your prof hear you talk the talk. Increase the length of your sentences in his or her presence. Ask questions using the right words. The fact that such behavior makes you a well-educated individual is beside the point. What you want is that silver bullet recommendation letter.

The long haul also allows you time to get into the original literature on your chosen subject. When combined with the jargon vocabulary, a familiarity with the original literature absolutely nails that recommendation letter. As indicated elsewhere in this book (see chapter 6) original literature is research that is published in scholarly journals. Knowing the publication dates, authors, and main conclusions of half a dozen pieces of original literature is a big time plus. Again, of course, just by knowing this material, you'll end up better educated. If actually becoming a well-educated person is a problem for some reason (maybe your significant other or best friends can't stand to be around well-educated people) then develop some ways to hide your accomplishments.

If you're going to outwit your prof by doing research then why not double the fun by outwitting your boorish friends, too, convincing them that you can be just as boorish as they are? I'd suggest some ways to disguise your newly-found abilities and power but I don't know your boorish friends as well as I know my fellow profs and besides, these suggestions might take some of the fun out of the outwitting game. However, regardless of how boorish you might need to act in order to be part of your particular in-crowd, I strongly recommend drawing the line before your boorishness descends into various lethal mixtures of alcohol, automobiles, and sex with strangers. Nevertheless, you obviously have some options in this game of outwitting various kinds of people for fun and profit.

[81]

Closure:

Projects always need to be brought to closure, not only for your own benefit, but more importantly because such closure gives profs enormous satisfaction, the latter, of course, being one of the prerequisites to this silver bullet recommendation letter. In writing this chapter, I realize that I've used the term "silver bullet" several times assuming that modern college students know what it means. If you've been plugged into truly ancient TV re-runs then you can probably skip this short digression.

Back in the 1940s, a radio show called The Lone Ranger aired weekly and in the 1960s there was a TV serial version. In this show, every week The Lone Ranger, a masked man on his "great horse Silver," along with his "faithful Indian companion Tonto," solved various problems for common people. The problems were typically ones of crime, corruption, passion, and ineptitude, although sometimes illness, nature, and bad luck played important roles. At the end of the show, The Lone Ranger would hand the now-saved victim a silver bullet then ride off. The fortunate recipient of The Lone Ranger's help would always ask, "who was that masked man, anyway?"

The silver bullet thus became somewhat of a symbol for big problems solved. The Lone Ranger never failed at anything, thus my use of the term "silver bullet letter" that never fails to open a door for students. I listened to The Lone Ranger faithfully as a kid. Eventually I came to believe that the best part of the show was the musical score, borrowed from Rossini's *William Tell Overture*. At the time I listened raptly to the adventures of The Lone Ranger and Tonto, it never occurred to me that I'd need a letter of recommendation for anything. The music, however, was downright thrilling and served as my introduction to classical music, as well. If that experience sounds familiar, in general terms, of course, then you may be destined to become a prof rather than spend your years trying to outwit one or more of them.

Back to closure. This event can take many forms, but the most common one is a paper of some kind, the format of which will depend greatly on your project area. In the sciences, papers are often relatively short, especially so if intended for publication because it usually costs money to publish scientific works and profs try, like everyone else, to minimize their costs. In the humanities, project papers are likely to be long and have extensive literature reviews and lengthy bibliographies. In some cases you may have to produce figures, which means learning to use some graphics software. Statistical analysis is a common requirement for papers. You may have access to some project reports written by your prof's former advisees, and if they are available, not only study their formats as models, but ask your prof questions about them. Remember, profs love questions about their work just like grandmothers love questions about their grandchildren.

Other forms of closure involve making a presentation of some kind, usually at a scholarly meeting. Yes, profs go to meetings, sometimes even large international ones, where fellow scholars gather to talk about their latest work and ideas. When they attend such meetings, profs may spend some of their evenings carousing the local bars, but they'll sit for hours in hotel chairs listening to other profs and their students make presentations. Nowadays, these short talks are always accompanied by Microsoft Power-Point graphics. Students who present in my classes routinely use this software, too.

If you end up bringing your project to closure through presentation, expect to travel, put together a short (10-15 minute) show of your project, and rehearse repeatedly. You'll end up in front of an audience, sometimes a large one, and you may be asked some tough questions. Nicole's experience of speaking in front of my large BIOS 101 class (200+ students), as told in chapter 12, will be of help in this case.

The most extreme form of closure involves an oral exam, especially if you're applying for a degree with distinction or honors. If you're in that category then you probably should be reading *War and Peace* instead of *Outwitting College Professors*, but I greatly appreciate the fact that you've gotten this far in chapter 7 and maybe you can recommend this book to a friend who really needs it. To continue, however, in the case of an oral exam, a committee will assemble somewhere to deliver the test. You might be asked to make a short presentation, similar to the one you gave at a scholarly meeting, just so the examiners will be reminded of what to ask you about. Then they'll start asking questions. The main point of these questions will be to discover something about which you're somewhat unsure. That "something" probably will be the subject of the rest of the exam.

What you'll really get out of a project:

In general, projects done by college students are, in and of themselves, fairly unimportant if not downright useless. So the point of such projects is not to win a Nobel Prize or make anyone rich or famous. The point is to give you an experience that cannot be attained except through serious independent study. Such experience routinely provides transferable skills. Years after you've completed it and filed your paper away with other college memorabilia in boxes your mother wants out of your closet now that you've moved away, you'll be using those investigative skills.

Final take-home message:

A project is a major commitment—of time, of emotions, and of a certain flexible kind of loyalty. You will get nothing out of a project, personally, without the commitment of time and emotions. Likes, dislikes, and some indefinable internal connection are what keep scholars working on projects for a lifetime; unless you get captured because of similar emotions, you are not likely to commit the other required resources. The loyalty comes from believing that your association with a particular prof is of personal value beyond whatever immediate benefits may come out of it. But in the end, you will end up learning how to learn, probably the most valuable take-home lesson available from any university.

8. Social Occasions and Etiquette

Beauty without grace is the hook without the bait.

—Ralph Waldo Emerson, 1860, *The Conduct of Life*

I get the impression from our campus at least that the last thing in Hell students want to do is end up encountering a prof socially. Nevertheless, it happens, and furthermore, contrary to popular belief, social events are prime venues for outwitting. So learn to take advantage of them! Here is a list of common and typical social occasions in which college students and professors encounter one another:

(1) "Meet your prof" nights at Greek houses and dorms

(2) Receptions of various kinds

(3) Graduation

(4) Bars and restaurants

(5) Getting invited to a professor's home

This list is arranged in order from the most difficult setting in which to outwit a prof to the least, although students probably believe it is arranged from least to most stressful. Getting invited to a professor's home is very likely the most stressful for students because so few of you can imagine it happening and I suspect nobody ever talks about it at freshman orientation. So I'll begin with the invitation to a prof's home then work my way through the more difficult ones like graduation and contrived occasions, including "Meet the Prof" night at your dorm, fraternity, or sorority.

I've arranged the above list in reverse order—from most difficult to easiest—because such an arrangement makes for easier reading and writing of this chapter. But one statement can be made about all these occasions: They are ones in which the student has all the power, period. And when the student has all the power then the prof is a real easy target, maybe one that's even asking for it.

(5) Getting invited to a professor's home:

Getting invited to a professor's home is a no-brainer outwitting opportunity, so if it happens, you need to be prepared. Why, you might wonder, would a prof invite students to his or her home? (Notice I'm using the word "home" instead of "house".) The answer is very simple: the prof feels an obligation to his or her students, enough of an obligation, in fact, to foot the bill for whatever treats are supplied. Furthermore, he or she trusts invited students not to break furniture, track in mud on her new carpet, get him arrested for serving alcohol to minors, or burn cigarette holes in the upholstery. In other words, you're being treated like both a friend and an adult.

So the first rule when invited to a prof's home is: *act like both* [friend and adult]. When some prof decides you are worthy of being treated both as a friend and as an adult then he or she has already done 90% of your outwitting job for you. This section is intended to help you with the other 10%. The second rule, which I'll repeat below, is a simple one: *know when to leave.*

[88]

I'll save the preachy-sounding advice about conversation and table manners for the end of this chapter because although it's important, it sounds too much like what your mother tried to teach you for the first 18 years of your life. You probably already have a mother somewhere; what you need now is a co-conspirator (me, through this book). So I'll start with the basics and work my way up toward the more advanced (= subtle) social skills a typical college student needs to finish the outwitting a prof has started, and largely accomplished for you, with the invitation.

Your first task is to respond to the invitation, either yes, I'll be there, or no, I have another obligation. RSVP stands for "*répondez, s'il vous plait,*" a French phrase that means "reply, please," or more literally "respond, if you please." The French ending, in this case (-*ez*) is actually an imperative form, that is, a command. So if you've been invited then respond, the minimal common courtesy to this person who is going to give you a grade this semester or write a letter of recommendation for you a year from now.

Your second task is to find out whether your prof is married and your third is to find out what other students are going. Usually the latter is quite easy to discover, because the invitation itself is likely to be addressed to a particular group—an honors class, a small group of students working on a project, a group of employees of which you are a member, etc. If there are several students, and you can arrive simultaneously with a couple of them, that's a good move. Faculty members are always afraid students won't show up to a social event, so are relieved when they appear in groups, even if the group is only two. Such arrival sends the message that you two (or more) have actually given some thought about the occasion and made some plans to attend. Any evidence for such thought is quite flattering to most profs. Surprised? You shouldn't be; profs' lives are typically devoid of flattery, even minor amounts.

[89]

If your prof is male and is married, and if his wife is present, which she will be if the guy has any class at all, and especially if she is actively involved in the social occasion, again which she will be if she has any dignity and is generally treated like an equal at home, head straight for her, introduce yourself, and thank her for the hospitality. If she's still messing around in the kitchen, offer to help (if she has any sense the offer will be declined).

At some point, after food and drinks have started being served, be sure to ask her where to put dirty dishes, paper plates, used silverware, beer cans, etc. Although that seems like a trivial act, remember that you are in her home and that this home is usually the one place where she is absolute ruler. Then, during the course of the evening, do the same thing in her home that you would do in the prof's office (see earlier chapters), namely, find something interesting to ask about or comment on, for example, art, children's pictures, quilts, or particularly difficult music left on the piano. When the evening is over, again thank her, and him, for the hospitality (but thank her first), and send her a thank-you note.

If your prof is a female and is married then the etiquette depends entirely—100%—on what kind of a person her husband is, how his wife interacts with him, and how comfortable he is with the situation. In the best of all worlds, the husband acts like his wife would act in the reverse situation, taking responsibility for some of the evening's plans and helping with food and drinks. This man may also be a prof (increasingly likely in today's society), in which case the first question you should ask is what department he's in unless you know that already. Then follow the simple rules set out above: talk to him about something in his field of interest, don't let him languish in the corner, and thank him when you leave. If your prof is female then a thank-you note is absolutely required.

[90]

(4) Bars and restaurants:

Students encounter profs rather commonly in bars and restaurants, especially in college towns, mainly because both students and profs frequent such places, and students often work in them. The absolute first rule for when you see a prof in this situation is: *recognize and speak to him or her first.* Whatever you do, don't let this person look at you suspiciously, as if he or she remembers you from somewhere, while you're ducking and diving, trying to avoid getting noticed. Even if you failed this person's course, recognize and speak to him or her first. Retain all the subtle humanistic power that dignity provides an individual; show yourself, if none other, that you are above pettiness, hard feelings, and recrimination even if you made an F.

In the forty-six years I've been a prof, I've given out almost 20,000 grades, 300-350 of them Fs. All of the students who received an F earned and deserved it. Some of those 300-350 people have gone on to successful and productive lives that make mine look rather pedestrian. I encounter a lot of my low performers in eating establishments. Biology teachers have a standing joke: "All my former students are either doctors or bar tenders." Not long ago, however, I went to a social gathering where the bar tender recognized me and spoke first. I made that wise crack about doctors and bar tenders. The young man told me he'd just be admitted to med school. I obviously got some mileage out of that conversation.

Having recognized your prof in a bar or restaurant, now what do you do? The answer to that question depends entirely on your particular role. The prof didn't come to that establishment to have conversations with students; he or she probably came there to get away from students. So here is the advice, based on your role:

a. <u>You're the bar tender or server</u>: Pretend you're at the prof's house and make some small but very intellectually interesting talk, especially if about a class, or how the semester is going. If you are the server at a restaurant, flatter this person a tiny bit every time you're at his or her table, but do it with dignity. Don't hover or bother this customer continuously about whether the meal is okay, even if management requires such behavior. In other words, convey the impression of recognition and respect but not awe. Your tip may be correlated with how well you perform this task. Figure out some kind of body language that makes people believe you're a waitress or waiter just for a short while on your way to becoming president of Harvard.

b. <u>You are both patrons with companions</u>: If it's in a bar, a casual hello and a throwaway question such as "How's the semester going" will suffice. If it's in a restaurant, and you have a nice looking date (male or female), introduce the prof, especially if he or she also has a date of the sex opposite from yours. If you're with your parents, you've just been dealt the Ace of Spades. Introduce your folks and make some comment about how interesting this prof's class was. Adjust your level of conversation and dignity to fit the establishment.

c. <u>You are both patrons without companions</u>: Assess how much this prof has had to drink and who he or she is with. If he or she is with a bunch of department colleagues and grad students then say hello, drop a few small talk words, and go on about your own socializing. If none of the other profs in the group get recognized by their students then you've scored significant points with very little effort. Let your prof initiate further conversation, and if he or she does then stay connected until you have flattered him or her enough in front of his or her colleagues. If the prof is a guy sitting alone over his third

[92]

shot of Jack Daniels at the end of the bar, be careful. If your prof is a female, alone in a bar or restaurant then you have a challenge and I'm not convinced I have an exact answer for you. In either case, however, a simple hello is a must.

(3) Graduation:

Graduation is the one college experience that is relatively standardized, at least in the United States, and among the most standard features is the expectation—on the part of both students and faculty members—that the occasion will be pleasant and in some mysterious way satisfying, regardless of how boring a commencement speaker might be. The profs are usually happy. They may relish going to graduation because it's a solemn and professorly event, or they may hate it because they are ready to be doing their own creative activities now that the school year has ended. But they all *know* that they will see lots of former students as well as many people who do not usually visit campus. They also know that there will be mostly students' relatives among those strangers at graduation because nobody goes to college graduation ceremonies just for entertainment.

Outwitting rules applicable to graduation are exceedingly simple (see list below) and there are only three. But why would you want to try to outwit a prof at or after graduation? The answer is obvious: because you could easily ask him or her for a job recommendation within a few years. Here are the three graduation ceremony rules that apply to any prof who you might need to ask for a favor in the future:

a. If you're a campus leader and get to give a speech, mention at least two profs, preferably those you may want to ask for a recommendation in the future.

b. If you happen to bump into the prof, and you're with your parents, immediately say excitedly, and loudly enough for the prof to hear, "Oh, Mom! (Dad!, or Mom and Dad!), I'd like you to meet Dr. _____!" then grab his or her arm and don't let go until you've introduced your parents. If there are younger siblings along, introduce them, too, and say something about them being future students in this prof's classes.

c. Any time that you find yourself close enough to a prof so that your eyes meet, smile and say hello. If appropriate, thank the prof for his or her help and for teaching an interesting class.

If you end up encountering profs at graduation and one of the three rules above does not apply then don't worry about trying to outwit this person. Neither of you will likely meet, communicate, or need the other again except in some highly unlikely and contrived situation like you see in the movies.

(2) Receptions of various kinds:

What kind of a reception might you attend where you'd encounter a prof? The answer: events held by student organizations, academic department functions, open houses held by offices in which you work, and social gatherings held in association with athletic events. The advice in this case is very easy to follow because it's a scaled-down version of that given for visiting a prof's home (see above). Say hello, make some small talk (preferably about academic matters, good books, recitals, art, etc.), and disengage gracefully.

Receptions of the type described, however, are the one case in which it's okay to use sex in a mild sort of way. If you're an attractive female and the prof is male, linger a little bit longer with him, or introduce him to an equally attractive female companion. But both of you need to say

[94]

something intellectual. Sexiness alone never—or at least very rarely—works with profs no matter how lecherous they may seem to you because profs tend to get bored in the absence of what they consider interesting conversation.

If you're an attractive male and the prof is female, do the same thing, but choose your intellectual topic rather carefully. I suggest art, music, or literature instead of country music or NASCAR. If you're not good looking enough to use sex to make an impression then accomplish the same thing with some interesting talk. As indicated elsewhere in this self-help book, in the vast majority of cases, physical appearance is subordinate to language and ideas. That relationship is manifested very strongly at colleges and universities where profs are not very good looking themselves and spend most of their time with what they sincerely believe are big ideas (whether they are or not, and mostly they are not).

(1) "Meet your prof" nights at Greek houses and dorms:

In general, this situation is a stressful one for both students and profs, but especially the latter, because they have little or no control over what happens at these events and they feel the burden is on them to accomplish something they're rarely good at, namely small talk. So if you know that you're going to end up at a table with a prof, at some stressful contrived event, and especially a prof that you don't know then have a list of starter questions handy. This list is pretty simple, but students seem to not think about such conversation starters, probably because they don't spend much time with strangers. Here are some hints:

a. Talk about an interesting class you took (not an interesting prof, unless it's the one you're talking to!) then ask the prof if he/she knows about that class. Profs usually love to talk about school, so this one is a sure fire conversation starter. If you've read in the student newspaper about some news such as a hiring controversy, a sexual harassment case, a tenure denial lawsuit, be sure to bring up that subject. Profs hate academic politics but they love to talk about it more than anything else. If you're lucky enough to have one of these cases at your institution, starting a conversation about it may result in a whole lot of insider gossip that probably should never enter student ears. If this happens, your "meet the prof" evening is a smashing success.

b. Some non-fiction book that you've been reading, especially one that is close in subject matter to the prof's area of interest.

c. Anything in the news that is anywhere close to the prof's area of expertise.

d. The prof's family (but be careful to do this in a subtle, neutral, way; this individual may be in the middle of a nasty divorce).

e. However, if this is a prof that you've invited then both the burden and the opportunity are yours. Everything that has been already said in this chapter applies. Act like this person is your date (he or she is), although a rather platonic one, of course. Whatever you do, don't let the conversation lag. But most of all, ask questions. Profs love to be asked questions, so oblige them.

Preachy-sounding advice about manners:

I joined a fraternity once, although left after a month. The first time I went to a pledge meeting, however, I was taught table manners: how a place is set, where the knives and forks go, which silverware to use when, how to eat soup, how to hold my knife and fork, how to put a piece of food in my mouth, what to do with my napkin, and a dozen or so other details. It was a bunch of guys telling me these things.

For some reason, at the time, it seemed like these table manners lessons had something to do with impressing women and/or future clients, so I listened. Since that time I've spent a reasonable amount of time with students who were eating. My former fraternity brothers were right: most guys need table manners lessons. So if your social encounter with a prof involves food—which is usually the case—and you are a manners-challenged guy, just watch the nearest well-dressed woman over the age of 40 and copy her eating behavior.

Final take-home message:

Social encounters with profs are occasions just made for you to practice outwitting skills. The rules for engaging profs in social interactions are simple, but depend somewhat on the setting. Nice table manners are always a plus, even for impressing dates and future business associates. But remember that in almost every social occasion, all the power belongs to the student, so use it!

9. Letters of Recommendation

I pray you, in your letters,

When you shall these unlucky deeds relate,

Speak of me as I am . . .

—William Shakespeare, 1605-06, *Othello*

Most college professors write dozens, if not hundreds, of recommendation letters every year. This chapter contains the inside information on how to ensure that the one some prof writes for or about you is a good one, although the advice may sound more like "How to be a good college student" than some students might want to read. Nevertheless, there are tricks to this business, and a student needs to know them.

At the end of this chapter, I've provided a couple of actual letters of recommendation from my files, with the names changed, of course, and some minor details altered because individuals would easily recognize themselves if I mentioned the exact subjects of their projects or the species they studied. I suggest reading these letters and deciding which one you would like to have written on your behalf. Both letters concern biology majors, and in both cases the students were applying to medical school, but the same general kinds of letters could be written by almost any prof in any subject area and addressed to any business or professional school.

[99]

The first rule in seeking letters of recommendation is so obvious that it sounds downright dumb, but you'd be surprised how many students violate it. That rule is simple: *if you're going to ask profs for recommendations, choose the ones in whose classes you've done well and who you believe have a favorable impression of your abilities.*

Duh. What students don't always understand, however, is that there are a great many ways to impress profs, and grades are only one of them. So from the very start of your college career, begin building relationships with those professors who seem to enjoy interacting with you intellectually, and allow, or even initiate, conversations about subjects beyond a particular class or a couple of points on the last exam. As a minimum, say hello to these profs on campus sidewalks. If you have any excuse whatsoever for contacting such people once in a while then do so. For example, it's appropriate to take them a newspaper article that you can honestly say you felt was important because of what you learned in class. Such behavior always works to your benefit, especially if done in semesters after you're no longer in this person's class.

The second rule is one that many if not most college students violate regularly, often to their later regret, and that is *make sure all your profs know your name early in the semester, are reminded of it regularly, and can recognize you outside of class.* Some profs will tell you this rule is actually the first one, and in fact it does go hand-in-hand with rule number one. If the only thing a prof can say about you is "he/she made an A in my large freshman course and seemed to always be courteous and well-groomed" then you've missed a major opportunity to outwit someone. On the other hand, if this class had 350 people in it, and the prof knows or believes that you were courteous and well-groomed then that's progress. At least the person knows how you dress, how you interact with fellow students, and where you sit. He or she could, of course, be lying.

The third rule is fairly simple, but again, many students ignore it, and that is *make sure your prof knows exactly who this letter goes to, the individual, the complete correct address, and if appropriate, has an addressed, stamped, envelope (supplied by you) to contain it.* Make absolutely sure the prof knows the deadline. If you provide a prof with envelopes, always type the address. Typically, however, profs write letters on school letterhead, so envelopes are not all that necessary; they are, however, a small courtesy. And the last rule is to *follow up the letter request*, just to make sure the prof actually wrote it.

It's always acceptable to either simply give your prof something in writing to remind him or her of who you are and what you've accomplished, or ask whether he or she wants such information. Personally, I greatly appreciate receiving a manila envelope containing a letter from a student giving me all the correct address information, deadlines for various applications, a two or three page résumé, and addressed stamped envelopes with no return address on them. I do most of this letter writing at home, so can simply stamp my professional return address on the envelopes, put the letters in, and mail them on the way to school.

Many recommendations nowadays are done online, and that kind of submission is likely to increase in the future. In this case, be sure that the prof has all the information he or she needs to submit the letter accurately. I appreciate it greatly when students remind me of the submission deadline, and I usually tell them to hassle me unmercifully so that I get those online submissions done in a timely fashion.

A final rule is one that probably should go in the Advanced Outwitting chapter because it involves the sometimes arcane world of academic politics, although only slightly. This rule is as follows: *if you have an option then seek letters from the highest-ranking profs that fulfill all the above criteria.* A person who moves up through the ranks of academic employment often starts as an undergraduate researcher then attends graduate school, receives a PhD, works as a teaching assistant, and sometimes spends a few years doing post-doctoral research before applying for a faculty position. If they're lucky and persistent they will end up getting hired at a college or university, and if they're really lucky, they'll end up with you—a student determined to outwit them—in their class.

Young, untenured, profs typically hold the rank of assistant professor for up to 6 years. They're not really "assistants" in the commonly defined sense; they are real profs but the term "assistant professor" is a traditional term for beginners. If and when they get promoted, these profs then become associate professors. If an associate professor performs up to a certain level for several more years, he or she will likely be promoted to full professor.

Full professors who distinguish themselves in some way are often rewarded with named professorships or endowed chairs. Thus if you have a prof whose official title is, for example, "The XXXX Distinguished Professor of YYYYY" then that individual has achieved the highest rank that a prof can gain without becoming an administrator of some kind. The XXXX usually denotes names of big or famous donors. Named Distinguished Professors usually sign letters with their full titles because they're proud of their accomplishments, sort of like a military officer wears his or her medals. This signature block—which can have a major positive impression on readers, especially other faculty members on medical and law school admissions committees—is the reason to select senior professors for writing your recommendation letters, if they'll do it and if you're confident in your class performance.

In general, the larger the class, the easier it is to make an impression on a prof. I said that earlier and it still applies. On the other hand, the larger the class, the less likely a prof's letter of recommendation will carry major weight in a selection committee's deliberations. In a typical case, you are in a large class in some subject you will never encounter again, at least as formal coursework in college, but you're doing well in the course and are thinking about applying for a scholarship. So you'll need a recommenddation. If you've dressed reasonably modestly from the first day, and if you've introduced yourself more than once, the stage is set.

The next class day, show up a little bit early and as the prof walks down the hall, look up from your student newspaper, smile, and say "hello." On the next class day, work up the courage to ask some meaningful question at the start of class, especially if the prof asks whether there are any questions. You can begin your question by saying "a few of us were studying the other night and . . ." Of course you may not have been studying at all, especially with friends, but the prof doesn't know that and he or she is enormously flattered to even think it would happen. The next week you can ask for the recommendation.

At the other extreme is a situation in which you have actually done a project of some kind under a prof's direction (see chapter 7). It matters little whether the project was an individual or a group one. What truly matters is the extent to which you as an individual have demonstrated the traits that recommendation letter readers look for when making scholarship or admission decisions. Unfortunately, such readers tend to look for evidence of those traits that we often see as boring. No med school admissions committee ever smiled favorably on an applicant described as "highly creative in speech and clothing, unbound by convention, and inclined to constantly challenge paradigms" regardless of the fact that many college professors appreciate such traits. Instead, a letter referring to someone as "responsible, courteous, able to bring a project to closure, and capable of leading a diverse group of people while keeping conflict to a minimum" usually will impress at least some committee members. The project is an ideal way to build this last kind of letter in your prof's mind.

However, now that I've tried to turn you into a good Boy or Girl Scout, I'll also offer some insider advice that could easily make a major difference in your life. *Always, whenever you have the opportunity to demonstrate some originality, especially if done in a dignified sort of way then do it.* I may have said this before, and if so then pardon the repetition, but the observation is worth repeating. Profs get so much of what both they and society appear to want—courtesy, responsibility, safety, obedience, hard work, and formula writing—that any deviation from this boring expected norm can work in a student's favor. But the deviation has to be done in a legitimate way.

By far the best opportunity for demonstrating originality is provided by assigned papers. Although I've mentioned this fact before (see chapter 6), it's worth mentioning again because of the often-assumed close relationship between writing skills and one's overall potential in almost any discipline. Indeed, most profs who have been in the business for any length of time have read thousands of pages of student writing and tend to remember what happens to their better students. So regardless of whether there is a statistical relationship between writing skills and later professional success, I'd (almost!) bet a semester's tuition that such a relationship exists in many profs' minds. My advice is to exploit this perception.

Let's assume that your papers are grammatically perfect and written in a style that would make your English teacher proud. How do you add originality to this already perfect essay? The answer is easier than you might think. Original observation, supported by tangible evidence, almost always works. Regardless of what you're writing about, just ask, then answer, the questions: What do I personally believe is the proper interpretation of these facts? and, What kind of evidence would support this interpretation? I suspect it will not matter if your conclusions are different from what you believe the prof wants. What that prof very likely wants is your own work rather than his or her, or even the text's, conclusions.

I recently had the opportunity to serve as chair of a committee to completely revise the undergraduate experience at my university, at least in the area of what many call "general liberal education." We opened up an online discussion board for campus-wide input; any student or faculty member could simply log on and make comments about university coursework and educational ideals, the only condition being that postings could not be anonymous.

The online campus-wide discussion quickly attracted a hundred or more participants, many of whom responded to comments posted by fellow students. In reading through these postings, I was constantly reminded that students tend not to distinguish between the various contexts in which they must, or choose to, communicate. Thus bar talk, banter at athletic events, and casual conversation in dorm hallways all use colloquialisms that may not be appropriate for a discussion about grades held in a faculty member's office. Similarly, cell phone text messages tend to be unpunctuated and devoid of grammatical form. When such communications are put up on online bulletin boards for all to see then the distinction between venues becomes blatantly, and in some cases embarrassingly, obvious.

The bottom line is that one of the most effective ways to increase the quality of your recommendation letters is through language you use in communications with your prof. Recognize when you need to be formal then be formal, both in writing and in speech. If you write and talk like an uneducated slob around your friends then do so with the clear understanding that your friends are giving you a free-bee that a potential employer will not. In this case profs are like employers. If you're going to ever ask one for a recommendation then always (*always!*) speak clearly, using correct English, and write in complete, grammatically correct, sentences.

Final take-home message:

Eventually, all of you will need letters of recommendation, and that need might come sooner rather than later, especially if you are applying for scholarships. The tricks required to improve the quality and impact of such letters are not very exciting but they will work to help you open doors, so it's a good idea to start using them your very first semester at school.

A couple of sample letters:

Letter #1:

Dear Admissions Committee Members:

This letter is to support the application of Ms. _____ for admission to _____. I have known Ms. _____ since the spring of ____, when she was a student in my BIOS ____ course. BIOS ____ is a majors core course that requires four papers in addition to exams, pop quizzes, an extensive laboratory notebook, and extemporaneous writing assignments. The course usually enrolls about 100 people, and they are virtually all majors, so I do learn my students' names early. In addition, I visit labs regularly, and communicate weekly with lab instructors, so I get to know the students reasonably well.

Ms. _____ was an excellent student in both lecture and lab. She also received extra credit on three of the four papers, indicating that she consistently displayed insight and depth, as well as writing skills, beyond those of her classmates. My records indicate she was rarely if ever absent from class. She is exactly the kind of person I would welcome into my laboratory as an undergraduate researcher. Personally she was always courteous, confident, and pleasant. I have no reason whatsoever to question her integrity. On the basis of her performance in my course, I expect her to become a successful _____.

Sincerely,

John Janovy, Jr.
Varner Professor of Biological Sciences

On the surface, the above letter is a good one, because there is nothing negative in it. On the other hand, this letter fails to address certain qualities that Ms. ____ may possess, and that could easily help her achieve her life goals had she demonstrated those qualities.

The letter that follows is also a positive one, but because of what the student has accomplished in her time at college, this letter could easily carry far more weight than the one above. But remember, if Ms. _____ in the letter above gets a letter like the one below from another prof her overall file will look pretty competitive.

Letter #2:

Dear Admissions Committee Members:

This letter is to accompany the application of Ms. _____ for admission to _____. I have known Ms. _____ for about two and a half years, since she was a student in my BIOS ____ course. BIOS ____ is a majors' core course that requires four papers in addition to exams, pop quizzes, an extensive laboratory notebook, and extemporaneous writing assignments. Ms. _____ made an easy "A" in BIOS ____; she also gained extra credit on three of the four papers, an indication that her work was not only superior in preparation, but also revealed intellectual maturity and insight beyond that of her fellow students. I tried to recruit her for the summer field program, but her summers have been fairly occupied with _____. In the year after the BIOS ____ course, Ms. ____ approached me about undergraduate research opportunities. I gladly accepted her into the lab.

All undergraduates who work in my lab do projects on _____. There is an almost inexhaustible supply of such problems, most are manageable by students with fractured schedules, many have fairly significant conceptual importance as models for _____ in general, and all are excellent learning devices because students can take possession of their projects completely, struggling with all the logistical issues until they bring it to closure with publication or presentation. Ms. _____'s project involves _____. This project is of evolutionary importance because _____. She will end up with a very nice paper, one that is easily publishable in a peer-reviewed journal.

Ms. _____ is exceptionally mature for an undergraduate. She exudes confidence and is perfectly at ease with faculty members and graduate students. She is not at all intimidated by difficult questions. In the lab, she learns techniques quickly and applies them easily, is responsible and clean in her use of common facilities, and exhibits safe behavior in all instances. Her data set is developing into a very large one, and although the organisms themselves are not always as cooperative as she would like them to be (typical of these species), she is patient and persistent in her work.

She also meets weekly with me and my graduate students and discusses not only science, but also subjects outside biology with comparative ease. Like all the students who work in our lab, she has been in our home on social occasions and has engaged in easy conversation with everyone about a variety of topics. She is certainly patient and tolerant of a wide diversity of people. I have never seen her angry or depressed, and her conversation about other people is always positive.

In summary, I believe she will become a truly superb health care professional and I would trust her completely as my family physician.

Sincerely,

John Janovy, Jr.
Varner Professor of Biological Sciences

10. Advanced Outwitting

There was only one catch and that was
Catch 22, which specified that a concern
for one's own safety in the face of dangers
that were real and immediate was the
process of a rational mind.

—Joseph Heller; 1955, *Catch-22*

Periodically students encounter profs who represent extreme cases; that is, standard methods of outwitting may not work on these people, and in fact might be counter-productive. This chapter is intended to help you survive your encounters with such types, although to be completely honest, it's really in your best interests to avoid them altogether if possible. But it's not always possible to schedule around these kinds of profs, mainly because they sometimes teach required courses, and periodically students end up in their classes quite by accident or because of inadequate information. So proceed with caution.

In contrast to my previous advice, the techniques in this chapter are not guaranteed to be successful. Profs who require advanced outwitting range from the outright dangerous to burnt-out cases who are not dangerous but can easily affect your transcript in a negative way. I'll begin with the truly difficult cases.

DANGEROUS TYPES, BE ALERT AND BEWARE:

1. The terminally insecure prof:

This person is dangerous but probably does not realize it at all because he or she is often delusional to boot. These folks often are manipulative spoiled brats, always having to be right and always having to stand in judgment of those over whom they have power (e.g., you). There are *lots* of these types in academia; indeed, academia may attract them, although the upper reaches of professional athletics are also well populated by similar kinds of people.

The key to outwitting these types is to relinquish only the absolute minimum amount of power needed to complete the task at hand and to always—*always!*—maintain your dignity and self respect. To be specific, never suck up to these kinds of people, never show any emotion, never let them see you sweat, and never, *ever*, get into an independent study course or any other kind of ongoing subordinate relationship with them. Keep a very low profile, answer test questions the way you believe this person wants them answered (usually a pretty easy thing to achieve because such profs often are incredibly transparent), and say "thanks" when criticized.

You may be dealing with real bullies here. Don't succumb to the temptation to actually contribute to class discussion, even when encouraged, except in two circumstances: (1) participation is graded and required, and (2) everyone else is doing it. Give these profs only what it takes to accomplish the class requirements, and never show them your more creative, innovative, or speculative sides.

[112]

Save these contributions for your terminally secure teachers (see below, in the non-dangerous list).

The key to recognizing a terminal insecure type is to study very carefully what happens the first time a fellow student asks a question. If the prof's response is highly authoritative then be alert. If he or she smiles, or otherwise seems to get some kind of personal satisfaction out of his or her own answer at the end of the response then really be alert. If he or she seems to be talking around the student's question and still seems to be getting that personal satisfaction then that's a serious red flag. And if you have an uneasy feeling that this person is getting almost sensual pleasure out of answering the question (rubbing up against the podium, rubbing his or her hands together, hands in pockets, etc.), but still is not saying much that you personally feel is of value, the fire alarms should be going off.

The daytime soaps are actually pretty good training for learning to recognize these types. Television soap operas depend on terminally insecure, manipulative, characters that cannot be trusted with power, and as a consequence these programs reek with body language and tone of voice. Thus if you can get beyond watching soaps for sensual pleasure and mindless diversion, they can be quite useful as a free lesson in recognizing some of the worst cases among the professor ranks. Once you get out into the business world, you might also encounter some of these characters, but they'll be easily recognizable because they are supposed to inhabit the realm of commerce and law. But some of the above rules will always apply: never let them see you sweat, never suck up, and never allow yourself to be vulnerable to their whims.

2. The ultra-feminist female/lecherous male:

Any prof that exhibits obvious gender bias—positive or negative—is a problem for students of the opposite sex and sometimes of the same sex. The first rule in dealing with these types is to keep your own sexuality suppressed in any formal encounter with them. If you're a male dealing with a university professor who is also an ultra-feminist, and have to go to her office for any reason, find a really smart but average looking girl to go with you and dress conservatively with no message-bearing t-shirts and certainly no hat, regardless of whether it's on straight. That way you'll not only fit the prof's stereotype of you (not as smart as women) but also avoid the threat that beautiful girls always pose to older women.

Regular (instead of ultra-) feminist profs are not really dangerous, and in fact they usually have plenty to say that the average guy should listen to, including comments about salary differentials, macho politicians who like sports, male professional athletes who father children in various cities, and institutional harassment policies. In contrast to an ultra-feminist prof, a regular feminist prof might teach you things that will help save your marriage or deal successfully with your two teenage daughters years after you've graduated.

If you're a female trying to deal with a lecherous male prof, and have absolutely no choice but to visit his office then always take a female companion with you, hopefully a very nice looking one. This combination will provide both consternation (because there are two of you, and two women together are a formidable challenge, especially if they seem to be friends) and pleasure for the guy (because your companion is a babe, which he'll appreciate, as well as the fact that you brought her to the encounter), and the result will be neutralization of his worst tendencies. He'll still act lecherous, but in a mild sort of way.

But in the company of these kinds of older guys, remember to always be with another woman who is obviously your good and trusted friend. On the other hand, the old-

[114]

er the lecherous prof the less dangerous he is mainly because he's probably seen careers of some fellow profs get destroyed by inappropriate gender relationships in the workplace. But the general rule is that women in groups are rather formidable, even in groups of two, so if you're worried about some lecherous old prof, always take someone with you to a meeting.

Homosexual profs should be handled with extreme neutrality, not because they're going to make a pass at you (good way to lose their jobs), but because they could easily be extremely intelligent, highly literate, and especially sensitive to all kinds of social issues, the latter because often they have been on the receiving end of society's general negative reaction to homosexuals probably since puberty.

It's a rare case indeed, however, when homosexuals on the faculty are dangerous; 99.9999% of the time they are more concerned with society's attitudes toward them, their partner, and their gay friends than with whatever you bring to the encounter. If you know they're gay then treat them as human beings, carry on a normal conversation with them, and you'll be just fine no matter how uncomfortable you are because of conservative religious upbringing, immaturity among your influential friends, or other reasons. If you don't know they're gay then whatever advice I give is irrelevant.

3. The really incompetent prof with no interpersonal skills:

More of these types inhabit the hallowed halls of academia than you realize. Most students give their profs a whole lot more credit than many of them deserve, the main reason being that students need and want decent grades. Thus the prevalence of this type of prof is usually greatly underestimated. I often hear students talking about profs of this type, but in mildly irritated terms, or sometimes even in amusement.

There is no reliable way to outwit these types; they don't have the human qualities that allow outwitting, not because they're so smart or cunning (which they may well be), but because they don't know they're incompetent and don't care anyway. Just stay away from them as much as possible and do your job in the classroom. If you have to interact with them, focus completely on the subject matter, the coursework, assignment, or whatever business you need to conduct and don't even try to be friendly, curious, or creative in their presence. They don't understand these latter traits, so your efforts at being an interesting person are probably wasted.

THE NOT-SO-DANGEROUS BUT NEVERTHELESS DIFFICULT TYPES:

1. The highly organized or paranoid prof:

I don't have any real data or statistical analysis to support this impression, but it really does seem like paranoia and obsessive organization tendencies often occur in the same individual, at least in academia. The first general rule in working with such people is to remember that their paranoia and obsessive behavior dictate the nature of all (and I do mean *all*) interpersonal relationships, no matter what those relationships might be, including, probably, intimate ones you don't know anything about. The second general rule is to allow a lot more time for whatever you're trying to accomplish with these people than you would with a less paranoid and less pathologically organized prof. Patience is the key; if you are not patient with these kinds of profs, they will react negatively toward you.

On the positive side, however, rest assured that whatever problems you have with paranoid and obsessive profs, those problems are but a small fraction of ones they have with themselves. Anything that threatens their highly structured lives produces emotional stress, and in extreme cases may actually render them ineffective at their jobs. So whatever you do, don't disrupt their schedules, or, for that matter, the arrangement of papers on their desk. Paranoia and obsessive tendencies can indicate some underlying mental illness, but if a prof has been around for a while then he or she is probably not so ill as to be dangerous to himself, herself, or others. Just be patient with these people, give yourself plenty of time if you have any official business to conduct with them, but when it comes time to ask for letters of recommendation, avoid them like the plague.

2. The full-of-himself (FOH) prof:

I have never met a full-of-herself prof, so the sexism here is probably close to being justified. These types are far more irritating than they are dangerous, but they're also very easy to handle. The technique is simple: ask them something that makes them feel like an authority then shut up and listen for a while. FOH profs are also highly vulnerable to positive or complimentary comments about their personal lives, so take a look around the office and see if there is anything that would let you make such a comment.

FOH profs are likely to have dogs as pets, instead of cats, because dogs give people unconditional love, whereas cats tolerate and exploit their "owners." So if you see a picture of a dog, you're really in business. Just say something like "what a beautiful dog!" and sit back while the guy tells you about his obnoxious Irish setter. Get a sad face and sympathize if there is a veterinary issue.

But no matter how friendly the encounter, don't ever ask for a letter of recommendation from one of these profs.

Only in rare cases can they bring themselves to say something positive about another person, and such positive comments about others, if dissected carefully and put into context, tend to reveal a self-serving motive. So if you have official business to conduct with this type of prof, come prepared to flatter him a little bit as part of the meeting, and also allot enough time so that he can tell you about himself and whatever he's doing that's important. Then thank him when you leave and don't come back unless you have to for some legitimate and compelling reason.

Positive advanced outwitting:

If you recognize that a professor is extremely intelligent, well educated on a broad range of subjects, highly literate, and sensitive to all kinds of current social issues then you're in luck. Not only is this person just asking to be outwitted (although he or she knows it and uses this trait as a teaching device!), but he or she will also turn you into a much better citizen, far more well-educated, than you would otherwise be, all as a result of your outwitting attempts. In other words, you're likely to turn into a literate and socially sensitive individual just by trying to pull the wool over this prof's eyes. Here are some subject areas and quick advice about how to use them:

Art:

Have a favorite painter or sculptor and know why this artist is your favorite. If you have some additional information about this person, or have been to a place either used in paintings or used by the artist as a studio then be sure to have such information at the tip of your tongue. Ideally, if you have a favorite then you ought to be able to also talk about a few others, related either in time, geographical area, or subjects. If there is any art hanging around campus in public places—student union, various classroom buildings, administrative offices—then be sure

[118]

to take note and be able to say something halfway interesting about the pieces.

Music:

The above advice regarding art also applies to music, although you should be able to deal with classical, rock, hip-hop, and possibly folk or bluegrass. Classical and folk are often a problem for most college students, so you may have to do some self education. Avoid country at all costs unless you're at an agricultural or vet school.

Popular culture:

Start analyzing popular culture, from cable news to soap operas, cooking shows, ESPN, and several sitcoms. By "analyze" I mean be able to talk about their subliminal messages, their structure, editing, choice of subjects, and effects on unsuspecting viewers—that is, everything we might call "meta-content." Watch for an occasion in which this kind of information makes a positive contribution to the conversation then use it, but sparingly.

Macroeconomics:

The key here is to be able to relate major economic phenomena to your daily life. Complaining about gasoline prices won't cut it; being able to say two complete, analytical, and rational sentences about the relationship between Middle East political events and the plight of American truckers will. And yes, fuel prices will, eventually, go up from where they are today.

Advertising:

The literary structure of TV advertisements is always a great topic. Analyze them the same way you'd analyze a short story for your English Comp class—what is the situation, who are the characters, what problems do they have to solve, how can they solve these problems in thirty seconds, etc. As for print ads, look for cases in which their messages are contrary to the common "good." The delusion that all women should either look like a super-model or be considered obese is a good example of a subliminal, and some would argue not so subliminal, message provided by so-called women's magazines at convenience store check-out counters.

Sports:

Look for something beyond win or loss, something that reflects on the human condition, and in which sport is simply the metaphor. If you can find this metaphorical situation in women's athletics, so much the better.

Sex:

For college profs, sexual attitudes of other cultures, especially when combined with religious beliefs, are usually pretty good conversational material, but only if the subject comes up naturally within a discussion of some other topic. Don't be embarrassed or self-conscious about sex talk, but keep it fairly clinical and to a minimum.

Religion:

In any discussion of religion at a college or university, keep it analytical. It's always a good idea to have some knowledge about the subject, but religion in general is such a vast body of information that there is no way to be really well educated unless you are a college professor yourself. Questions about religion are always well founded, but again, in an analytical mode. Never get mad if someone affronts your religious sensitivities, *never*.

Background information on academia and academics:

In general, students know very little about how academic institutions actually work, and often faculty members are equally naïve. Most of the time this ignorance is harmless, and excusable, but at other times it suddenly becomes important for a student to know how a system actually operates. If you find yourself mystified by what's happening to you at college, especially at a large university then this section might be of help.

I can't solve personal problems, of course, so that if "what's happening to you" involves alcohol, drugs, automobiles, sex with strangers, gambling, and other kinds of self-destructive behavior, all in various combinations then you need more help than you can find in these pages. But if "what's happening" involves some strange mysterious and subtle communications with people you believe really ought to be acting like responsible adults then maybe I can help. In reading through the following paragraphs, remember that throughout this book I've used the term "prof" mostly in a very general way to refer to anyone who is teaching a college class. Now we'll take a closer look at these folks.

The first thing to know about academia is that people who teach classes fall into many different categories based primarily on the nature of their contractual agreement with the institution. Instructors and lecturers may not hold a PhD, and even if they do, they may not be employed in tenure track positions, also called "tenure track lines" because such a position will be identified by a line number in some budget spreadsheet. "Track" actually means "on track to get tenure if he/she performs well enough."

In academia, the term "instructor" is often an official title that defines the contractual agreement between teacher and institution. The word "instructor" also is a generic term, but universities don't always use it that way. Instructors are not necessarily expected to do research, unless they are graduate students, then they must do research, and do it well, or ultimately fail at achieving their life goals. In-

[121]

structors, in the contractual sense, however, can be paid a pittance and denied access to benefits like group health insurance. They are cash-saving devices and their morale can easily reflect their situation unless they are graduate students, in which case they might actually be proud and happy to be cheap labor doing what they love, believing that a satisfying "life of the mind" future lies not too far ahead.

The term "assistant professor" does not mean "assistant" but instead refers to the lowest rank among university employees in tenure track positions. Assistant professors usually are not tenured; if they are, then they are actually glorified cheap instructors and could easily be burnt-out cases. You should always check your university's web site to see exactly who your teacher is and what kind of information is readily available about this individual. Assistant professors should look young and happy in their web site pictures, although if they're in front of a very large audience in an introductory course then by the time you see them in person, they're probably terrified instead of happy, unless they are natural-born performers, and then they're likely to be on a little ego trip that works to your distinct advantage.

Young untenured faculty members are often under extreme pressure to do research and do it well, hopefully well enough to get a grant and bring money into the university. This description is especially applicable to scientists at larger institutions. Unless such young profs produce publications and earn a reputation as a scholar within five or six years, they'll get fired (denied tenure) at the most vulnerable time of their lives, usually regardless of how thrilling they may be in front of an audience. Thus the terror.

Any student in a class taught by a terrified young untenured assistant professor should be careful, although that student has been dealt an ace. Such frightened faculty

[122]

members are easily outwitted, and often greatly appreciate your efforts, but they can also be highly protective of their time, so that whatever tricks might work well on a seasoned old prof could well backfire when tried on one of these young types.

"Associate professor" is a title that refers to someone who is tenured, but mid-career and still working on his or her reputation as a scholar. Newly tenured associate professors are usually relatively young, and depending on their personalities, they may treat their tenure as a great relief or as an excuse for displaying a whole lot of pride in themselves. Watch out for the latter types. Again, check web sites; any associate professor, especially at a mid- to large-sized university, should be in his or her late 30s to early 50s, happy, confident, willing to interact with students, but at the same time somewhat protective of his or her research time.

Full professors generally fall into two categories: the senior scholars who may be generating massive amounts of grant money, especially in the sciences, and senior scholars who don't give a damn about grant money because they've demonstrated that they are good intellects and thus feel free and confident in that self-awareness. Some of these senior scholars will also be in disciplines that traditionally do not have access to grant money, good examples being philosophy and English. Senior faculty members usually have seen everything that students can throw at them, from the proverbial "dog ate my homework" to deaths, serious illness, automobile accidents, snow storms, floods, electrical failures, computer crashes, etc.

Older profs often don't care about student excuses because they've discovered that it takes more time and energy to enforce rules than it does to subvert those same rules in some way that is of benefit to a student. So if you absolutely must have dealings with older faculty members then

[123]

don't be too shocked if they treat you as an adult and tell you to get on with your class work. But if they seem intent on reprisal or punishment, be warned: they may be in one of the really dangerous categories described above.

Final take-home message:

Academia serves as a home for some really dangerous types, profs who can have a major negative impact on your entire college career and perhaps even on your chances of a good job afterwards. Learn to recognize these types and avoid them if possible. Academia also provides a haven for some truly wonderful profs who are happy, intelligent, and excited about their jobs and their interactions with students. Learn to recognize these kinds, too, and cultivate them.

11. Get a Job

Where they hung the jerk that invented work.

—Lyrics from "The Big Rock Candy
Mountain" – American folk song.

There are two rules about jobs, rules that have been revealed to everyone in higher education during the past
twenty years, everyone, that is, except students. The two
rules are: (1) whatever job you are going to college to
quailify yourself for could easily not exist by the time you
graduate, and (2) there are likely to be a hundred new *kinds*
of jobs available by the time you graduate, jobs that you
are not thinking about now and for which you are not going
to be qualified by virtue of your college education. These
two rules are a product of the information age, the human
migratory patterns that blossomed into national crises by
the early years of the 21st Century, and widespread military
and cultural conflict.

I may be wrong about the assertion that students have
not been informed of these rules. It's entirely possible that
all students everywhere have been told these rules over and
over again and have simply refused to believe them. Alternatively, parents of students, that is, people who should
have learned these rules by now from having lived them,
especially during the last half of the 20th Century, do not
believe they apply to their children. Grow up, kids, and tell

[125]

your folks to grow up, too; with very few exceptions, the rules—especially the second one—apply to you.

Before going on to the serious and important stuff, I'll dispense with the exceptions, namely, jobs that cannot be outsourced and are not likely to disappear during the next decade because of information technology. Here is a brief and illustrative, although incomplete, list of such jobs and careers: barber and hairdresser, real estate agent, funeral home director, tax attorney, auto mechanic, nurse, dentist, shoe salesperson, local pharmacist, physician, estate and real estate lawyer, and professional athlete.

Obviously there is quite a difference in earning potential between a first round NBA draftee and your local barber, but these two professions share a common property: they can't be done via the Internet from Bangalore. On the other hand, at least some of them can be done by people who, unlike you, have no investment whatsoever in an American college education. These jobs—like all jobs—also can be turned into rich and rewarding careers, but such transformation depends far more on an individual's attitudes toward self, life, liberty, and the pursuit of happiness than on any college degree.

Outwitting College Professors, of course, assumes that you've already committed yourself to a college education, so this chapter is intended to help you fool profs into aiding your efforts to lead a rich, rewarding, and productive life long after you've left their classrooms. That is, you want a *career* instead of just a *job*. What is the first thing you need to know in order to accomplish this rather intangible goal? The answer to this question is very simple: you need to know what kinds of experiences actually produce rich, rewarding, and productive lives.

You also need to know that such experiences do not necessarily involve frequent trips to the bank in order to

[126]

deposit major amounts of cash. Instead, they are most likely to involve aid to those less fortunate than you, personal creativity, in-kind contributions to your community, public service, close friends, and visual and performing arts, perhaps in various combinations. In other words, richness and satisfaction are derived mostly from internal sources, not external ones. Although that assertion may sound more like what you might find in some inspirational literature than in a book about outwitting a college prof, the claim nevertheless is well founded and your own community probably abounds with perfect examples to support it.

Professors have more access to enriching and rewarding experiences than you might believe at first, and furthermore these folks usually don't have to be outwitted in order to share that access with you. In fact, most profs are more than ready to tell students about all kinds of opportunities, for example, internships, concerts, exhibits, speakers, needs for volunteers, and really unusual part time jobs that might not pay much but provide the rough equivalent of a second major.

An excellent example of the latter is a position held by a college junior who worked as a textbook assistant in my office. I am one of the authors of a leading science textbook (*Foundations of Parasitology*) that gets revised every four years. Such revisions involve about a year and a half of almost full time work. Much of this work is something that virtually any bright college student with a longer than average attention span could do, for example literature searches, writing permission letters, finding good pictures, etc.

By the time we finished this latest revision and turned in the manuscript, the young lady who spent 5-10 hours a week at minimum wage was conversant with much of tropical medicine and economic entomology from having read about 10,000 abstracts of scientific papers, reviewed them with me, and honed her information processing skills to a level far beyond that of her peers. Although washing glassware is not particularly educational, part time jobs such as that held by the student who helped with my writing are, and furthermore, they provide a person with perspective, vocabulary, and maturity not available through regular classes.

Regardless of how rich and rewarding your personal life may be, however, eventually you will need a roof over your head, a living wage, and access to transportation. Depending on your personality a stable relationship with a significant other can sometimes help in your pursuit of happiness and statistics show that happily married men live longer and healthier lives than unmarried men. Women, on the other hand, statistically speaking, seem to be able to get along without men better than men can get along without women, especially in the case of women with good jobs.

So back to the subject of *your* job, the one soon to become your *career*, the excellent high-paying one that you are now preparing for by taking art history, English literature, and sociology because some adviser told you that those courses were "required" but which you fervently believe are an absolute waste of your time and tuition. My goal, of course, in writing this chapter, is not to get you that first job, but to get you the second, the promotion, and ultimately the career. Unfortunately, for those with narrow and highly focused vision, it's the so-called "general education" or "liberal education" part of your curriculum that is your best avenue to that promotion.

As it turns out, you are not alone among students in feeling that required liberal education courses are a waste of your time and money and that you should be focusing your resources on activities that will lead to immediate employment (accounting, teacher certification, advertising and marketing). But we have data that show such an attitude is simply wrong. The Association of American Colleges and Universities (AAC&U) does research on important issues facing today's post-secondary institutions then conducts workshops, summer institutes, and meetings to address those issues. AAC&U also generates publications and provides consultants and visiting experts, including their own officers.

A few years ago the AAC&U President at the time, Carol Geary Schneider, visited the University of Nebraska-Lincoln where she delivered a major presentation entitled "General Education; Liberal Education: Promise and Practice" and in which she summarized the history of and e-merging trends in American higher education over the past century, the results of student focus groups (of both high school seniors and college juniors and seniors), and the educational accomplishments that employers also want to see in their new employees.

According to the students in these focus groups, the most important outcomes of a college education are time management skills, maturity, self-discipline, and teamwork training, whereas the least important ones are tolerance and respect for other cultures, civic responsibility, computer skills, and ethics. Specific knowledge—history, statistics, physics, Shakespeare—was nowhere on the students' radar, yet subjects such as these are the hallmark of a "truly educated person," that is, the kind of individual who should be occupying positions of importance in our complex society.

Why should any person in a position of power be "truly educated"? The answer is simple and is found in the old familiar quote (or some version of it) from the philosopher Georg Wilhelm Friedrich Hegel: "What experience and history teach is this—that people and governments never have learned anything from history, or acted upon

[129]

principles deduced from it." An alternative version ("Those who don't learn from their mistakes are doomed to repeat them.") is nowadays used in many different contexts, ranging from team sports to military conflict, but most tellingly by employers. Now that you've paid your first semester's tuition, it's time to take a different look at the so-called "general liberal education" courses; they are one long lesson in how humanity has dealt with Hegel's rather cynical, but widely admitted, judgment of people and nations, especially those that fail because of willful ignorance.

In addition to the AAC&U publications, there also is an important and valuable web site sponsored by the National Survey of Student Engagement (NSSE) program at the University of Indiana, a program that includes not only student , but perhaps more important for our purposes, a Faculty Survey of Student Engagement (FSSE). Reports from this program are readily available online (see http:// nsse.iub.edu) and provide a rather sobering, but hopeful, picture of college and its potential impact on a student's career options. On the hopeful side, the 2014 NSSE Report indicates that ~26% of all seniors were doing research or independent study under the direction of a faculty member, and that number is 46% for liberal arts colleges offering only a baccalaureate degree.

These numbers mean that *somewhere between a fourth and a half of all college seniors are actively engaged in learning how to learn, the key to long-term meaningful employment*. On the sobering side, a few years ago, ~30% of all freshmen did "just enough academic work to get by." Your goal, from the perspective of long term meaningful employment, is to move from the latter group into the former; in other words, get off your butt and learn how to learn—*anything and everything*.

[130]

Other NSSE data from a few years ago also show surprising results, and furthermore reveal that college students routinely engage in activities that employers know contribute to an employee's ability to navigate a changing and challenging world. Nearly 80% of freshmen said that they "often" or "very often" wrote papers that required integration of ideas from multiple sources; by their senior year that fraction approaches 90%. Well over half of these students "incorporated concepts from different courses" when doing writing assignments or engaging in class discussions. Nearly a third of these same students, however, indicated that they never attended a play, theatre performance, or stepped inside an art gallery. Nearly half never tutored other students, either voluntarily or for pay. Yet the performing and visual arts are a major economic and social driving force in today's world and teaching is widely known to be the most effective means of not only learning, but also learning how to learn.

What NSSE tells us is that colleges typically give lip service to equipping students for long, productive, and meaningful careers, but also provide opportunities for turning lip service into reality. Referring back to chapter 4 ("Small Talk/Big Talk"), as a conversation starter that has real potential for improving your employment options and survival skills, try the two questions: Are there students in our class who need and want help? and Where is the nearest art gallery (= When is the next play at the University Theatre?) Suddenly "outwitting" some college professor looks suspiciously like working with that same prof to engage in activities that you both know make you a deeper, more adaptable, multi-faceted individual (employee), i.e., exactly the kind of person who survives in the 21st Century global economy.

Employers, again according to national surveys, want information literacy, communication skills, creativity, intercultural awareness, ethical reasoning, and the ability to adapt existing knowledge and skills to new situations. In other words, according to available research, students today are focused on themselves and their own personal development to "maturity," but employers are focused on the global marketplace and the premium it places on innovation, flexibility, communication, and adaptability.

Your outwitting goal, therefore, is to convince some prof to help you achieve what employers want, and what you need in order to get promoted into a second job, or become so valuable you can't be downsized. Nobody, especially me, is guaranteeing you anything in the way of a long, successful career or a happy productive life. Everybody, including me, is pointing to international trends, global statistics, and the proven power of innovation as major factors that will influence your ultimate ability to earn a living, provide for a family, and lead a rewarding life.

Now, having said all of the above, which is admittedly a little bit idealistic, I should perhaps return to the reality of meaningful employment in the United States. Regardless of how much progress has been made by women butting their heads against the so-called "glass ceiling," there is still a decided male bias in corporate America. To quote national columnist Barbara Ehrenreich (TIME Magazine, July 31, 2006): "Among other things that have changed since the '60s is the corporate culture, which once valued literacy, numeracy, high GPAs, and the ability to construct a simple sentence."

In doing research for her book *Bait and Switch: The (Futile) Pursuit of the American Dream,* Ms. Ehrenreich discovered a job coaching industry that claimed "elusive qualities such as 'personality,' 'attitude,' and 'likability'" were of essential importance to would-be applicants and that "Play down the smarts . . . [the] self-help books advised, cull the experience and exude a 'positive atti-

[132]

tude.'" However, one of the anonymous reviewers of *Bait and Switch* on Amazon.com says "she failed to find a good job because, like many unemployed Americans, she was middle-aged and did not have well-placed connections."

Regardless of whether Ms. Ehrenreich or her reviewer has analyzed the American corporate employment landscape correctly, Ms. Ehrenreich does have a point when she concludes that "Someone, after all, is going to have to figure out how to make an economy run by superannuated slacker boys competitive again in a world filled with Chinese and Indian brainiacs."

Final take-home message:

If I have any final advice to young college student job seekers and career builders, it would be to always remember the famous Andrew Carnegie quotes:

Man does not live by bread alone. I have known millionaires starving for lack of the nutriment which alone can sustain all that is human in man, and I know workmen, and many so-called poor men, who revel in luxuries beyond the power of those millionaires to reach. It is the mind that makes the body rich. There is no class so pitiably wretched as that which possesses money and nothing else.

And

Surround yourself with people who are smarter than you are, get out of their way and let them work, then go out and brag about what they did.

You might want to be a millionaire (or, in today's world, a billionaire), but you don't want to be one who possesses money and nothing else; thus I recommend indulging yourself in the arts. Nor do you want to work for someone who is so dumb, so socially insecure, or such a bully, that he or she cannot get out of your way and let you

[133]

work. At most colleges and universities, profs are the very people who want you to succeed in the long term, if for no other reason than that such alums tend to write donation checks to their alma maters.

But remember that profs are teachers first; they are in the business of discovering and developing human resources. You are their raw material, the stuff from which they build their own rich and rewarding careers, not their enemy. When it comes to careers, remember also that you have four or five years to be a real college student and forty or fifty years to be something else. "Outwitting" these profs suddenly looks a lot like giving them something to brag about.

Finally, as you read through the next chapter, remember that you will be in your late thirties when Nicole's nephews and niece graduate. That is, you will be fifteen to twenty years beyond college. I have a personal story that may help put "fifteen years" into perspective, although it probably sounds like an eternity today. Here is the story:

In 1954, when I was a junior in high school, I convinced a reluctant girl friend that she should go see a grade B sci-fi movie entitled *Destination Moon*. Fifteen years later I was married (to a different girlfriend!), with two children, and on July 21, 1969, I took our oldest daughter by the hand, plopped her down in front of a black-and-white TV, and said "you have to watch this." "This," it turned out, was Neil Armstrong stepping onto the moon's surface and uttering that famous quote about one small step.

I assure you that whatever the date you are now reading this book, fifteen years hence you will be amazed, and perhaps bewildered, by how the world has changed. Nicole's letter is not only to her young relatives, it's addressed, whether she realizes it or not, to her peers, and to you.

[134]

12. Letter from Nicole to the Classes of 2029, 2031, and 2033

Words of wisdom to my nephews Caden, 5, Drew, 3, Carson, 3, and niece, Cameryn, 1

—Nicole Searcey, Class of 2012

"Congratulations! We are pleased to inform you that you have been selected for a US Student Fulbright award for 2012-2013 to Chile." (Institute of International Education)

I ogle the e-mail on my phone between classes; my eyes well up; then the levy breaks. My dumbfounded mind can only think, "I can't remember the last time I've been this happy." A few weeks pass then I receive more astounding news:

"Congratulations! On behalf of the U.S. Department of State, Bureau of Educational and Cultural Affairs and the Institute of International Education (IIE), I am pleased to inform you that you have been selected as a recipient of the Benjamin A. Gilman International Scholarship." (Institute of International Education)

Jubilation spreads through my body like the racing blood in my vessels, again obliterating whatever thoughts might have been in my mind at the time—"Are you kidding me? How in the world am I so lucky?" Within a month, I had just received two highly competitive, national scholarships and was on my way to Costa Rica, for five weeks of immersion Spanish, and then Chile, where I'd spend a year studying the parasites of mummies.

After receiving money for college, awards at scientific meetings, or heart-warming reviews from students whom I mentor or help as a Teacher's Assistant, a truly thankful and reassuring feeling arises: during the past four years of college, I must have done something right. Thus my letter to you—my niece and nephews; I want you to have the same kind of rewarding experience that I did at an American university.

Caden, Drew, Carson, and Cameryn, you have many years before deciding what college to attend, what to study, and where to focus your energy and attention, but now, as I'm sitting in the University of Nebraska student union and experiences of the last four years are parading through my memory, I wish to share some advice. My purpose is not to provide scholarship-winning tactics or show you how to build a stellar resume, but instead to help you find a passion and love for learning, whatever your interests may be. Scholarships and resumes magically materialize along the road your heart chooses, and my sincere advice, if you actually listen to it (you're not so good at this now, but I'm optimistic), will certainly help you achieve your goals.

Cameryn, everyone agrees you are a most charming and personable little girl. I love it when you laugh, and everyone around you is entranced by your lively blue eyes, curly blonde hair and porcelain-like chubby cheeks. Being social, cheery, and talkative are important skills for later in life too; and believe me, such skills are more important than most people realize. As you grow, please keep talking; converse with, and be outgoing to, as many different kinds of people as possible. Being shy will only hold you back. We live in a social world, and it's important to know how to act and behave in all situations, especially those involving your advisors, professors, or people in influential positions. You

[136]

never know if someday you'll have a chat on the bus or elevator with your future boss, co-worker, or even your spouse.

As you learn how to act in different situations, notice the different ways in which people live, and how their ideas, hobbies, and lifestyles differ. A quote by Francesca Farr explains, "Our view of reality is only a view, not reality itself." Our world is becoming ever more interconnected and diverse, and Cameryn, I doubt you will live on the farm outside Murdock, Nebraska, forever.

My attitude towards social and professional situations proved beneficial in college, and among the many things I gained from it was the unique mentorship of two influential professors. Most students, especially students at large universities, do not receive this type of guidance, and without it I would be much less successful than I am so far. Strive for this type of mentoring. These tips will guide your thoughts and calm your nerves in various situations, and hopefully your actions will mark you as a standout student that professors will recruit for research, undergraduate teaching, or various other educational endeavors such as presentations at scholarly meetings. These opportunities are especially likely if you follow your aunt's path and become a biology major!

Tips on behavior around professors:

Realize that all professors are not only professors, but they are family members, possibly parents, and they have hobbies and enjoy music. They were your age once and could probably even admit stories of stupid things done in college. Of course, you won't ask about these things (yet) because it's important to keep a professional relationship. In short, they are only human, just people like you and me. Never be afraid of faculty members; just don't!

If you do not have a question about class material or a typical reason to visit your professor's office hours, find one and go have a conversation. Your professors, at least the ones with a high outwittability profile (see Chapter 2), want to help you learn, discuss ideas and interests, and watch you mature intellectually. You might not realize it, but you need their guidance. Ask for this type of mentorship; don't be shy; and, go talk with them. Trust me, this kind of activity will lead to opportunities.

You can make conversations with professors very uncomfortable because of nerves or anxiety. I know profs can seem very different than yourself, but know you are in control of your feelings. You have the ability to stop being worried. Think about these things: Does anyone approve or enjoy your nervousness? Do you desire to feel this way? Does your prof want you to be panicky and uneasy? Who enjoys a conversation with a nervous, fluttering blabbermouth?

Before you enter your professor's office, close your eyes, avoid distractions, and imagine yourself sitting in front of your professor. Maybe she has grey hair, aging skin, and a daunting dialect. Her office is filled with books, artwork, and laboratory paraphernalia that you know so little about you cannot compose a question. You feel tense, completely out of place, and wish your parents could have taught you about some of these things growing up. You think, "This person seems so different than any other human being I know." Now, with all your mental will, give your reasons for being there:

- Even if I'm unfamiliar with the art, textbook material, faint music coming from the stereo speakers, or lab procedures now, I want to learn, and I am eager. I am only 18. I have plenty of time.

[138]

- I know most my peers aren't working up the courage or will to converse with this prof, and so I already have one-upped them.
- I should talk with my professors; yes, I am doing what I should be doing. I am holding myself to a high standard.
- So my only interests now are social media and partying, but I like biology, (insert your nerdy, secret interest you are embarrassed to admit to your dorm neighbors) and this prof is going to help me find a passion in something truly meaningful. The campus will get bigger than my dorm, and soon I'll find buddies with interests like mine.

If you are really determined to improve your social, speaking, and interacting skills around profs, turn on your cell phone voice recorder, stick the thing way out of sight, and after the conversation and recording listen to yourself talk. Also perform this little task if you are public speaking. Take note of your "umms," "likes," or rushed sentences. You are represented by your speech and language. If you don't present yourself in the manner you expect, you will portray yourself as less intelligent or capable than you really are.

In summary, never ever be afraid of profs, talk with them frequently, be confident in your reasons for being there, know why you should not be nervous, and practice your social and language skills all the time. Not only will you become expert at interacting with professors, but your skills will be transferrable and will help you interact with others in various situations, maybe during a job interview or conversation with in-laws.

Drew, you are a special little boy. Most noticeably, you are curious about the world around you. "Why?" is the most commonly used word in your vocabulary. Sometimes kids get less speculative and more obedient as they get older; it may seem easier to follow directions than to question or understand why they exist. I'm not suggesting you burn the rulebook, like you're doing now as a three-year-old, but it's okay to question the directions, events, rules, or assignments that will be a part of your college life.

As you go through college you will have experiences you don't understand, including outlandish assignments you think are a waste of time. My best advice is to ask yourself, "*why* did the prof assign this?" Put yourself in his or her mind, and decode what he or she was thinking. Professor A, "My students should be really familiar with finding sources in the library." Professor B, "It would benefit these kids to compose papers every week; their writing and vocabulary will improve." Even if you are really uninterested in, for example, the theoretical physics or advanced calculus books you're studying, complete the task for your own self-improvement. Your thought may be, "Next time finding sources in the library will be really easy," or "Yes, I just impressed my advisor with that new vocabulary word." Focus on the transferrable skills you will learn from completing the assignment. Always think about why it was assigned and why it will make you a further educated person.

After receiving assignments is not the only time to question the activities around you. Being inquisitive and speculative are good characteristics to express in general. For example, your advisor tells you to take the class History of Jazz because it will fulfill two degree requirements. It's okay to think "Heck no, let me pick a class that actually catches my interest" (no less to jazz music). Other examples: "Why is my prof teaching this large lecture in such an unconventional way?" Maybe she has done research in teaching. "Why does my prof have a humongous jaw bone sitting on the shelf?" Maybe he found it somewhere. "Why did my roommate fail organic chemistry?" She definitely went out too much.

After every inquisition, use your conclusion with wit, such as, "Hi Professor A, I really enjoy the unique way in which you teach lecture. I read a few of your papers in the Journal of Education." To Professor B, "I saw a picture of a similar looking fossil reading National Geographic, is this specimen rare?" To yourself, "shoot, I probably shouldn't join everyone at the movie tonight because I should study for my final exam tomorrow morning." Drew, take the time to reflect on your activities, never stop asking "why?" And, be witty if you can; use your questions to impress your professors.

Carson, I cannot remember the last time you sat still for even a short period of time. You love staying busy and engaging with world around you, and my advice is to keep this up! When I started college I was afraid to miss out on any valuable opportunities. I searched for interesting groups to join, applicable jobs, or whatever seemed to provide intellectual excitement. I was disheartened when I was rejected from some opportunities because I needed more experience, more classes, or needed to be 19. My freshman year resumé was bleak, but looking at it three years later, it seems I was an overachiever.

So how did my résumé go from blah to excessive? It mainly took time, so it's okay to be patient. For many positions you need a decent GPA to prove you are capable of more responsibilities. Thankfully my attitude and performance in freshmen classes (except maybe calculus!) made me positively different than some of my peers, and so opportunities started coming my way. If your prof suggests something, for example he writes a note on your graded paper that you should take advantage of an opportunity you know nothing about, be adventurous and open-minded. I have never regretted taking a professor's advice. Whenever I received an offer from a club, job, or teacher, I never said "no." One time I was having a meeting with an advisor and she asked, "How did you get involved in so many things?" My response was, "I didn't look for them; they all came to me."

So how do you get life chances served to you on a silver platter? You will probably be served unappetizing options first, and yes, it's necessary to accept them. For example, in my case, a prof asked me to practice lab techniques, unpaid, during the summer, in order to prepare for a class at a biological field station. This preparation was not required for my major, plus I was broke and should have been working, but since I attended that summer program and was a dedicated student, the prof followed up with an offer to fill his Teaching Assistant position—like it was served on a silver platter. I learned that first summer that if you don't say "no" to activities with profs or others in decision-making positions, eventually really great opportunities will be introduced to you.

Carson, please don't lose your engaged disposition, never be shy, and get involved with whatever interests you have on campus. Even if you don't initially enjoy such activities, learn as much as you can from them and hang on, because if you do them diligently and with a smile, there will be more opportunities to come. Plus you might get a really nice recommendation letter. Having a wide breadth of experiences is really meaningful and satisfying. Breadth is power because no matter what conversation you find yourself in, you will probably have something intellectual to contribute.

Caden, you are the head honcho of the Searcey kid pack, being the first one to graduate pre-school and all. You looked so handsome in your cap and gown, diploma in hand. Although I don't want to imagine you, your brother Drew and your two cousins Carson and Cameryn getting taller, older, and interested in things other than stroller rides, I know you all are growing fast and I know you will take on leadership positions as you continue your education, just like you are the Searcey kid leader now. I will share my opinion on what one learns from being in a leadership position.

Depending on the major you choose, and based on your obsession with Legos, it might be in the field of engineering, you will have different opportunities for leadership. My major was biological sciences and so I had the opportunity to be a teacher's assistant, laboratory instructor, and parasitology researcher. I was also a mentor and officer of the William H. Thompson Scholars Learning Community for three years. Satisfaction, challenge, dedication, and an "I'm actually important and making a difference in people's attitudes and lives" feeling developed from my experiences. The most transferable and significant personal skills that grew from my leadership positions were how to speak in front of crowds and the importance of attitude and appearance. In all situations, I strived for improvements in these skills.

I am particularly thankful for one public speaking exercise during my junior year as the BIOS101 teacher's assistant, to over 200 students for about forty minutes. I was asked to present my research project after recently winning the undergraduate student prize of $100, a plaque, and bragging rights at a scientific meeting. I was a smidge nervous as I waited to begin my lecture presentation, thinking "Woah! All these peers, some my age, will have their eyes on me and they will carelessly listen to me talk about monogenes." To a normal person, monogenes are very tiny, unimportant, and disinteresting parasitic flatworms that live on fathead minnows, another typically non-fascinating species, especially to freshman girls. No less to the girls, I just know that when I took BIOS 101, I was really more interested in the boys sitting in front of me than in worms.

As I unevenly shifted my feet in front of the lecture hall, I thought: "what rhetorical devices will make these students want to listen to me?" Even if they weren't interested in fish parasites, I wanted them to be interested in biology or something I talked about. Now I'm thinking at the time, "Aha! First, I must look personable. They might be interested in what I do if my appearance suggests I could be their friend." So I made another mental note, "keep smiling, Nic." Yes, appearance will help.

A cough from the third row while the prof was talking interrupted my reverie. "Okay Nic, why didn't you think about this stuff last night?"...hmm my subconscious blurted out to the attention center of my brain, "Be confident in your speech; I don't enjoy conversations with shy, timid people." I started to relax, knowing that the presentation would be more enjoyable for everyone in the audience if I acted confident and cool. Maybe I'd even convince some people that my research is fascinating and enjoyable. My subconscious chimed in again, "Wouldn't that be rewarding to influence the career path of any students listening to me? Nic, try and look extra cool in the name of science."

When the presentation was finished, all two hundred students wrote a handwritten page of text in class responding the topic, "What did you think of Nicole's presentation?" That night I eagerly started to read each page, excited to know the secrets in each person's head about my presentation and body language. The moon was out and it was late when I finished, but the responses were intriguing and I started a list of every criticism or compliment. I wanted my public speaking skills to improve, and I was determined to never make the same mistake twice. "You looked nervous, but not so much after a while." "You only made eye contact with the back of the room." "I still don't understand what a monogene accessory piece is." "Did Dr. Janovy and you plan to wear matching sweaters?" That coincidence and comment makes me laugh when I recall it.

Caden, as your leadership endeavors progress from master Lego builder and iPad controller to, why not, student body president and beyond, I hope you make every occasion a learning experience. I wasn't expected to make a list of criticisms after my BIOS101 speech, in fact I haven't even talked to anyone about that activity, but now I look or think about my notes before every presentation. It especially reminds me to not be nervous or say "umm." If you seriously reflect on what you've accomplished and strive for personal improvement in all of your leadership positions, you will learn a great deal more than ever expected. How to speak in front of crowds and the importance of appearance and attitude are only a few examples of what you are capable of learning while being in a leadership position.

Caden, Drew, Carson, and Cameryn, I know all four of you will be leaders in college. You already have big, unique personalities for having such high-pitched voices and little shoes. I hope my advice will be applicable and advantageous to your future activities. I care so much about you all and would love to be a part of every college experience. For this reason my counsel is written here, in hopes you will want to read it. You may think, "My aunt was a weird 22 year-old," or "what an over-achiever; I'm going to make fun of her now" but I needed to share my genuine thoughts about how to get the most out of your college education, making your days at any university very satisfying and enjoyable, because I wouldn't want you to live your lives in any other way.

Love you all!

Your Aunt Nicole

[145]

Num	Dept	Title	Cr	Grade
109	CHEM	Gen Chem	4	A
101	BIOL	Gen Biol	3	A
101L	BIOL	Gen Biol L	1	B+
150	ENGL	Comp	3	B+

13. How to be a Good College Student if You Really Want to

Cauliflower is nothing but cabbage with a college education.

—Mark Twain, *Pudd'nhead Wilson*, 1894

The Rules:

The rules for being a good college student are really very simple, and first and most important one of all is:

(1) **GET UP AND GO TO SCHOOL EVERY DAY**. Everything else is pretty much secondary in importance. The other rules are as follows:

(2) Make sure every instructor you have knows your name, and make sure that instructor knows you and your work well enough so that he/she can write a letter of recommendation for you if necessary two years from now.

(3) Simply decide today that you are not afraid of, or intimidated by, faculty members, no matter how obnoxious or wacko they seem, and regardless of whether their "values" or religious beliefs are consistent with yours.

(4) Pay attention to world events, especially those with a cultural component. Try to understand why these events take place, even though your courses may not deal with

[147]

anything other than specific subject matter having nothing to do with global politics or economics.

(5) If your campus or the town it's in has museums, visit them about once a week. Talk to your friends about what you see in those buildings.

(6) Pay attention to the campus landscaping; read the labels on the trees and plants. Talk about campus landscaping and vegetation with your friends. I know, this idea really sounds dumb but trust me, there are times and places where such conversation really pays off, and in a surprising number of cases, these times and places involve members of the opposite sex.

(7) Read some high quality magazines fairly regularly. I suggest *The New Yorker, Harpers,* or *Atlantic Monthly.* Ask your instructors for a reading list of non-fiction books and read some of the items on such lists.

(8) Talk to your parents or guardians about the ideas you are encountering at college. Make these folks believe that their investment is paying off. If you get an opportunity (e.g., at church when home for holidays) then practice this same idea-talk with other people your parents' age. Such practice will pay off in many ways, especially at job or professional school entrance interviews.

(9) Do *something* original and creative (poetry, music, sketches, etc.) on a fairly regular basis. This advice is especially important if you are not a fine arts major (if you are then you don't need the advice). So few people today either have or take the time for original work that anyone who does ends up developing mental skills that set him or her apart from the general public in a major [positive] way.

(10) Go to free lectures and recitals when you have the opportunity. Once you get there, stay through the whole

thing and be a quiet and attentive audience member.

(11) Talk to your fellow students. Find out who are the most challenging faculty members in the arts, humanities and social sciences, and enroll in those teachers' courses. The general rule in college is an important one: if given an option, *always take people instead of course numbers, **always***.

(12) Remember that the age 18-25 is the cheapest time to go exploring, make a mistake in your academic plans, correct it, move on, do something different, etc. Taking a big chance when you're 50 is a whole more expensive than taking one when you're a 19-year old sophomore and looking at a poetry class instead of organic chemistry. It's always a mistake, *always*, to let some professional adviser tell you exactly how to fill up your most wonderful, exploratory, and life-building years.

(13) Finally, remember it's the humanities that will give you a rich life well beyond college, not the technical courses in your major. Accounting and electrical engineering will maybe get you a job, but literature, philosophy, and art history will enrich your life immeasurably for the next 60 years after that first job which, if the statistics are true will be only one of several.

Applied regularly, these rules—which are actually behavioral practices—will turn you into a well-educated person in a hurry. They may also make you seem like a real nerd to some of your bubba friends, but their future is not yours. You and your parents, not your friends, are the ones paying for this college education. You, not your friends, are going to reap the benefits of this education. College is a time to acquire certain skills, to be sure, but it's also a time to start building a career for yourself.

So quit worrying about your friends unless you see them engaged in self-destructive behavior and believe that

[149]

you simply must try to help them. They may appreciate the help, but they may also tell you to butt out of their lives. That's how friends are, and later in life, you may discover that your spouse and children are, or at least can be, similar in this respect.

Self-destruction:

Self-destructive behavior among college students usually involves drugs, alcohol, automobiles, sleep deprivation, and sex with strangers, all in various combinations. I've mentioned this deadly combination before, but it's worth mentioning again. If you can get through your first year without succumbing to this suite of seductive pastimes then you're probably on your way to a fine education. In recent years, sexual assault has become recognized as a relatively major problem on various campuses. If your institution has assault policies, pay attention to them and protect yourself from danger in every situation, whether it be an off-campus party or a walk back to the dorm from a night class.

For the information age, I probably also need to mention video games, the Internet, your smart phone and text messages. These technological germs probably won't make you physically ill, but they'll have about the same effect, namely, depriving you of the time to pursue high quality intellectual endeavors. There are exceptions to this last comment, of course; for example, if you're good enough to make a fortune designing video games then it's probably okay to be involved in that business!

Suicide is not a common occurrence at American colleges and universities, but it does happen, and when it does, often people who have associated with the victim remember behaviors that suggested this person was deeply troubled. I strongly suggest seeking professional advice and help if you have serious thoughts of destroying yourself, or if you see fellow students who are acting in ways that suggest the potential for suicide. Deep depression, sometimes strengthened by failing interpersonal relationships, can lead to suicide attempts. So can a sense of irredeemable failure and guilt. All colleges and universities have offices and services that can help in emergencies or in times of great stress. I encourage you to find out where those offices are, and how to contact the assistance personnel, as part of your initial weeks at college. You may end up saving a life, and that life could easily be your own.

It's not healthy to deprive yourself of sleep. Doing so tends to alter your metabolism and cognitive functions in a variety of ways, none of them good. So sleep deprivation is fairly self-destructive, not only in the short term, but also over the longer time period when your transcript and intellectual skills should be carrying you forward to some kind of a productive life. That's why sleep deprivation is a primary tool for interrogation and torture by various military and law enforcement agencies. There is nothing more dumb than staying up all night studying for some chemistry exam (or any other exam, for that matter). You've probably heard that advice a million times, and the reason you've heard it so often is because it's true and people generally want you to succeed. Society as a whole is better off when its number of drop-outs is minimized.

Nor is it healthy to try to survive a grueling intellectual endeavor on a steady diet of pop, French fries, candy bars, aspirin, sugar, caffeine, grease, and beer. Over the long haul, eating well, and smart, is essential to good intellectual performance. I'm not going to champion any particular mixture of foods, except to say that all nutrition experts recommend a healthy dose of fruit and vegetables, some minimal amount of protein, a mixture of whole grains, and plenty of fluids such as water.

[151]

Study techniques and habits:

One of the first things a college student should do is start acquiring a repertoire of study habits and techniques applicable to various subjects. The way you study chemistry, for example, may not be the way you study art history. Thus the question you'll need to address is not so much "*what* should I know for this exam?" but "*how* should I acquire whatever I need to know for this exam?" The difference between *what* and *how* is a big one.

The better students always, and I do mean *always*, understand this difference. Knowing *what* you need to pass an exam gets you through the next exam; knowing *how* to acquire what you need gets you through a whole lot of other situations that may have nothing at all to do with that exam subject. Knowing *how* to acquire knowledge and skills gets you through life, whereas knowing *what* gets you only through the next crisis. We're actually talking about that old Chinese proverb: "Give a man a fish and you've fed him for today; teach a man to fish and you've fed him for a lifetime." You'll do best in college, and in life, if you'll learn how to teach yourself to fish.

There is no single secret to acquiring the right study habits. Everyone is, or at least could easily be, different in this regard. What works for one person may not work at all for another. But as a general rule, research on the relationship between long term success and standardized test scores tends to show that people with high verbal skills do best in the long run. So no matter what the subject, from electrical engineering to philosophy, language skills tend to pay off.

Mathematics is a form of language (although mathematicians may argue with this assertion), so that any subject that relies on math, especially heavily, also relies on a sequential understanding of relationships and ideas. Relationships, characteristics, and ideas may be expressed in symbols, but these symbols still convey information about options, boundary conditions, and properties. The last sentence could as easily apply to literature and art as to math. So language tends to be universal and "written" in a variety of media. That's why it is so important for a serious student to also be serious about words.

How do you become proficient in language? If I knew the answer to that question, I'd patent it, sell it, and buy a big yacht. I do know how *not* to become proficient in language, and that is to ignore completely the rules of spelling, grammar, and sentence structure, and to studiously avoid reading whenever you can. So I suspect the opposite behaviors will improve your language proficiency at least a little bit if not a lot.

You also have to remember that in the United States there is a language known as Standard English, which is actually a foreign dialect for many Americans. This language does not include many of the phrases you learn from the movies, and it certainly does not include the double negatives so commonly heard on television, especially out of the mouths of hero and role model athletes. Instead, it tends to be the language in which are written important non-fiction books and magazine articles, contracts, prenuptial and other legal agreements, and laws.

Film scripts and novels don't have to adhere to Standard English, and fiction writers routinely depart from that language to create mood or define characters. The important thing for a college student to remember, then, is when and why to use Standard English. The answer is whenever the situation and context demand it. A really good college student, however, is perfectly comfortable departing from Standard English, again whenever the situation and context demand it.

Information Age issues:

It has been said that the average American receives about 25,000 messages a day, many if not most of them unsolicited. Furthermore, this information, e.g., that being delivered by the cable news broadcast now droning on the big screen TV in the Student Union lounge where I am currently writing this paragraph, tends to come in the form of short statements of "fact" or opinion. My parasitologist colleagues draw an analogy between modern information technology and infectious agents: smart phones, for example, have infected the brains of young people and in so doing have changed those folks' behavior.

This idea sounds preposterous? Put your phone away and walk across campus and through some buildings where many classes are taught. Estimate the fraction of your peers completely absorbed by whatever is happening on that little screen. It's amazing, isn't it? That technology has indeed altered the routine behavior of your, and all future, generations. Want a big time outwitting trick? If I've mentioned this one before, it's okay because the trick is so simple and powerful:

> Put your phone away, walk to class looking around your environment, study landscape vegetation and your fellow students, and if you see a prof on the sidewalk, look right into his or her eyes, smile, and say "hello." Trust me. It works.

There is virtually no careful or thoughtful analysis on television, although Charlie Rose's interviews with famous actors come pretty close. At least you'll hear an hour's exploration of what it means to be a highly visible public figure, the "what it means" part varying, of course, with Charlie's guest.

Many of the segments on *60 Minutes* are also highly

[154]

analytical. But what generally passes for analysis, even on cable news shows, is quite shallow. In most cases, if you actually wrote out the discussion verbatim, you'd discover it's neither as extensive nor as well documented as your last required History paper was supposed to be. So most of you have grown up in an incredibly rich information environment that provides little or no default training in careful and critical analysis, that is, in those skills needed to actually be successful over the long haul.

How does one become an analytical and insightful person? I don't know for sure, but from watching thousands of students over the past several decades I suspect that this transformation can't be accomplished without practice. The easiest practice involves reading of serious non-fiction books. Any faculty member at most colleges and universities can give you a list of titles. Here is mine (distributed to lots of undergraduates), consisting of publications that have made a truly major difference in how I view the world, vote, conduct business, design my teaching, invest my money, converse with my family members, and interact with other people.

The first thing you'll notice about this list is that it contains none of the so-called "classics." The second thing you'll notice is that it contains one of my own, listed because it describes decision making and career-finding among some of the most wonderful people I've ever encountered (my former students).

Adler, M. 1982. *The paideia proposal.* Macmillan, New York.

Armstrong, K. 2000. *The battle for God.* Alfred A. Knopf, New York.

Bedau, H. A. 1987. *Death is different.* Northeastern University Press, Boston

Chidester, D. 2000. *Christianity: a global history.* Harper Collins, New York.

Currie, E. 1985. *Confronting crime: an American challenge.* Pantheon, New York.

Desmond, A., and J. Moore. 1991. *Darwin.* Warner, New York.

Diaz, T. 1999. *Making a killing: The business of guns in America.* The New Press, New York.

Dorner, D. 1996. *The logic of failure: why things go wrong and what we can do to make them right.* Henry Holt and Company, New York.

Dyson, F. 1979. *Disturbing the universe.* Harper and Row, New York.

Dyson, F. 1984. *Weapons and hope.* Harper and Row, New York.

Farb, P. 1968. *Man's rise to civilization as shown by the Indians of North America from primeval times to the coming of the industrial state.* Dutton, New York.

Farb, P. 1974. *Word play: what happens when people talk.* Alfred A. Knopf, New York.

Friedman, T. L. 2005. *The world is flat: a brief history of the Twenty-First Century.* Farrar, Straus, and Giroux, New York.

Fussell, P. 1989. *Wartime: understanding and behavior in the Second World War.* Oxford University Press, New York.

Gould, S. J. 1989. *Wonderful life: the Burgess Shale and the nature of history.* W. W. Norton, New York.

Halberstam, D. 1986. *The reckoning.* Morrow, New York.

Hertsgaard, M. 1998. *Earth odyssey: around the world in search of our environmental future.* Broadway Books, New York.

Hofstadter, D. 1985. *Metamagical themas: questing for the essence of mind and pattern.* Basic Books, Inc., New York.

Honigsbaum, Mark. 2001. *The fever trail: in search of the cure for malaria.* Farrar, Straus & Giroux, New York.

Hughes, R. 1987. *The fatal shore: a history of the transportation of convicts to Australia.* Collins Harvill, London.

Janovy, J. Jr. 1994. *Dunwoody Pond: reflections on the high plains wetlands and the cultivation of naturalists.* St. Martin's Press, New York.

Koestler, A. 1971. *The case of the midwife toad.* Random House, New York.

Kuhn, T. 1970. *The structure of scientific revolutions.* University of Chicago Press, Chicago, Illinois.

Kurtz, P. 1983. *In defense of secular humanism.* Prometheus, New York.

LeShan, L. 1992. *The psychology of war: comprehending its mystique and its madness.* Nobel Press, Chicago, Il-linois.

Lopez, B. 1986. *Arctic dreams: imagination and desire in a northern landscape.* Charles Scribner's Sons, New York.

Mailer, N. 1969. *Of a fire on the moon.* Little, Brown and Company, New York.

Mayr, E. 1982. *The growth of biological thought.* Harvard University Press, Cambridge, Massachusetts.

[157]

McNeill, W. H. 1977. *Plagues and Peoples.* Doubleday, New York.

McPhee, J. 1980. *Basin and range.* Farrar, Straus & Giroux, New York.

McPhee, J. 1989. *The control of nature.* Farrar, Straus & Giroux, New York.

Montagu, A., and F. Matson. 1983. *The dehumanization of man.* McGraw-Hill, New York.

Mostert, N. 1976. *Supership.* Warner, New York.

Pirsig, R. M. 1974. *Zen and the art of motorcycle maintenance.* Morrow, New York.

Power, S. 2002. *A problem from Hell: America and the age of genocide.* Basic Books, New York.

Reisner, M. 1986. *Cadillac desert: the American west and its disappearing water.* Viking Press, New York.

Rothschild, M. 1983. *Dear Lord Rothschild: birds, butterflies and history.* Hutchinson, London.

Sheehan, N. 1988. *A bright shining lie: John Paul Vann and America in Vietnam.* Random House, New York.

Shilts, R. 1987. *And the band played on.* St. Martin's Press, New York.

Sobel, D. 1999. *Galileo's daughter: a historical memoir of science, faith, and love.* Walker and Co., New York.

Steinbeck, J. 1941. *The log of the* Sea of Cortez. Viking Press, New York.

Sutton, G. M. 1979. *To a young bird artist: letters from Louis Agassiz Fuertes to George Miksch Sutton.* University of Oklahoma Press, Norman, Oklahoma.

Thomas, L. 1974. *Lives of a cell: notes of a biology watcher.* Viking Press, New York.

[158]

Tuchman, B. 1970. *Stillwell and the American experience in China.* Macmilllan, New York.

van Buren, P. 2011. *We meant well: how I helped lose the battle for the hearts and minds of the Iraqi people.* Henry Holt, New York.

Wilson, E. O. 1978. *On human nature.* Harvard University Press, Cambridge, Massachusetts.

Zinsser, H. 1934. *Rats, lice and history.* Morrow, New York.

Any faculty member who cannot provide such a list, regardless of whether it includes "classics" or not, probably should either be avoided or not taken too seriously as a role model. Failure to quickly come up with a suggested reading list indicates this faculty member is so stuck in the depths of his/her discipline, that he/she doesn't have a lot to say about survival in the next fifty years (which is what you have to do).

Time management:

Finally, there is some research showing that most of what a student learns during his or her first year in college is time management. Almost every college student you talk to will tell you this, so the claim bears a reasonable amount of truth. Time management is an essential skill because of the delusion that you have a lot of free time in college. If you have only a 9:00 AM and 11:00 AM class on Monday, Wednesday Friday, and classes from 10:00 to 2:00 on Tuesday and Thursday, then you have a whole lot of free time, right?

Wrong. You'll end up with a whole lot of assignments that break up your schedule; you'll be on the receiving end of about 25,000 messages a day in all media and they will shatter your concentration; and, there will be things that you want, or feel you need, to do (see the list at the start of this chapter). The problem with being a college student is not so much that you don't have time, it's that whatever time you do have is broken up into a lot of bits and pieces by the system.

Should learning time management be a major accomplishment for college students? I believe the answer is "yes." The information age is not going away any time soon. You'll be faced with time management issues for years well beyond your college days, too.

Finding a good adviser:

One of the students who read an earlier edition of this book suggested I add a section on finding a good adviser, so here it is, although not all institutions give you much flexibility in this regard. Probably the best advice is to remember that "advisers" are supposed to do two things: first, tell you whether you are making progress toward your degree goals (the requirement satisfaction function), and second, to give you unofficial suggestions about the rest of your life (the mentor function).

Most students confuse these two roles, believing that having accomplished the first, an adviser automatically accomplishes the second. The two functions, however, are quite separate and distinct. The requirement satisfaction function you can easily perform for yourself just by reading the college bulletin and asking a few questions. The mentor function requires quite a bit of insight into human character, as well as several decades of experience. What you really want to do relative to advising is find someone who will tell you the requirements to satisfy quickly and with authority, but then go find someone who will sit down and talk about all your options, especially those in which you must set your long term sights rather high.

Final take-home message:

Post-secondary education is expensive for an individual in many ways: time, money, and deferred life experiences such as marriage, parenting, etc. But a well-educated citizenry is an essential component of any free and open society. The so-called "average citizen", namely, the majority voter who also pays income, property, and sales taxes, is the safeguard of freedom and representative government. However, there is no "average" citizen in any nation, especially in the United States. Instead, there is a group of about 320,000,000 human beings who share both a set of living conditions guaranteed by a constitution and an almost overwhelming obligation, namely that of sustaining a civilized society with respect for the individual.

The civilized society is what is so dependent on people who can read, write, analyze situations objectively, understand economics, and appreciate the lessons of history. This kind of society also depends on people who are not afraid to use their education for the common good, even though that common good may not match completely their own recognized biases and beliefs. Your decision to obtain a college education is a costly one, for certain, but the cost of an uneducated public, especially in a nation that is highly dependent on science and technology, is much higher. If outwitting some college professor helps you achieve a life goal then this book has done some good. If by achieving that same goal, you also are helping to sustain the level of civilization to which we Americans have become accustomed then this book has done far more good for your nation than it has for you.

I wish you the best of success in college, and in your life after college!

Acknowledgments

First, I would like to express my deepest appreciation to those ~20,000 students who enrolled in my classes between August, 1966, when I started teaching at the University of Nebraska and August, 2011, when I retired. I would also like to thank the parents of these students for helping to support this amazing enterprise we know as American Higher Education. I thank you on behalf of those thousands of other faculty members and university administrators around the country who have not yet expressed similar appreciation to students and parents.

Second, to the people who worked in my lab for those same years, my heartfelt thanks for all those conversations about teaching, learning, ethics, and professional development. Those conversations often occurred in the most unlikely places, ranging from local watering holes and coffee houses to some van we were driving on a field trip to those special nights out at the Cedar Point Biological Station white gate. Especially important to the ideas in this book are the Crescent Moon Coffee House and Indigo Bridge Coffee House, the scenes of Friday coffee, mentioned elsewhere.

I also learned a great deal from students who ignored the advice in this book and ended up generating a lot of unhappiness for themselves and probably their parents. Watching another person screw up can be highly educational, especially if you recognize what's happening and apply the knowledge to your own situation. It's a shame that nations never seem to accomplish this simple task of learning from either their own or other nation's mistakes.

Strange as it might seem, I need to thank a number of my fellow faculty members, especially those whose behavior resulted in the "Advanced Outwitting" chapter. Some of you have provided truly wonderful lessons in how not to be a college prof, and in a few cases how not to be chair of a committee or an administrator, either.

Finally, special thanks to three recent students: Stephanie Bitzes, Nicole Searcey, and Nicki Everding. Stephanie was my office assistant during 2011-12, did extensive textbook work, and was the model for the victory sign image on the cover. Nicole was a student from my BIOS 101 class; she ended up doing research in my lab and in the lab of a colleague, eventually resulting in a Fulbright Fellowship to study parasites of mummies in Chile. I asked Nicole to contribute a chapter because she was near the end of her college career, had some young relatives she could use as a literary device, and happened to be around when the idea of a student contribution came up. Nicki did serious editing on this edition of OCP, in the process teaching me several grammar and punctuation lessons. Like many of those other 20,000 students, Stephanie, Nicole, and Nicki exemplify the rule that every college or university's most valuable resources walk in the front door, un-announced, every fall semester.

I know it sounds like shameless self promotion, but I firmly believe that if some institution would give every one of its new students a copy of *Outwitting College Professors* as part of the admissions package, that institution would be a significantly better one by October without the expenditure of a single additional dollar. In other words, just by listening to our students, and watching what truly works in terms of faculty-student interactions, we'd learn how to do our business very well regardless of budget and administrator agendas.

John Janovy, Jr.

Books by John Janovy, Jr.

Keith County Journal

Yellowlegs

Back in Keith County

Fields of Friendly Strife

On Becoming a Biologist

Ten Minute Ecologist

Biodiversity: A Primer

Dunwoody Pond

Vermilion Sea

Comes the Millennium (as Jack Blake)

Teaching in Eden

Foundations of Parasitology (with Larry Roberts and Steve Nadler)

Outwitting College Professors

Pieces of the Plains

E-books and Print-on-Demand

Bernice and John: Finally Meeting Your Parents who Died a Long Time Ago

The Ginkgo: An Intellectual and Visionary Coming-of-Age

Dinkle's Life: A Spiritual Biography

Conversations Between God and Satan

Intelligent Designer: Evolution for Politicians

Tuskers

Be Careful, Dr. Renner

The Stitcher File

The Earthquake Lady

The Author

John Janovy, Jr. has published over a hundred scientific papers, eleven trade books by major publishers, and the leading textbook in his discipline (*Foundations of Parasitology*, McGraw-Hill, with L. S. Roberts and S. A. Nadler). He has also written the script for an internationally televised film based on his books about the western plains (*Keith County Journal*, 1985, Nebraska ETV, 16mm and video, 58min; 1986 Corporation for Public Broadcasting, 1st place in local information programming category). His book subjects include natural history essays (*Keith County Journal*, St. Martin's; *Vermilion Sea*; Houghton Mifflin), high school athletics (*Fields of Friendly Strife*, Viking, winner of the *American Health* magazine book award for 1987), anti-intellectualism in America (*Comes the Millennium*, St. Martin's, as Jack Blake), and higher education (*Teaching in Eden*, RoutledgeFalmer).

He is the winner of numerous prizes for both teaching and research, including the University of Nebraska's Distinguished Teaching Award, Nebraska Libraries Association Mari Sandoz Award, American Society of Parasitologists Clark P. Read Mentorship Award, and the University of Nebraska Outstanding Research and Creativity Award. Dr. Janovy has taught large introductory science courses throughout his career; that experience, along with his several administrative positions and service in international scientific organizations, gives him unique insight into workings of higher education, especially those factors that affect student lives.

Web site: http://www.johnjanovy.com
Blog: http://fridaycoffee.blogspot.com
Twitter handle: @jjparasite
Follow John Janovy, Jr., on Facebook.